A JOURNEY THROUGH
OZ

Renee,

Ducks = $!
(see preface)

Chris Jesse

A JOURNEY THROUGH
OZ

THE BUSINESS LEADERS' ROAD MAP TO TRACKING INFORMATION TECHNOLOGY ASSETS

BY
CHRIS JESSE

RTP
Research Triangle Publishing, Inc.

Published by
Research Triangle Publishing, Inc.
PO Box 1223
Fuquay-Varina, NC 27526

The publishers have given permission to quote from the following
copyrighted works. From *MAN FOR HIMSELF* by Erich Fromm,
Copyright 1947 by Erich Fromm. Reprinted by permission of
Henry Holt & Co., Inc. From *The Lion of Boaz-Jachin*, by Russell
Hoban. Reprinted by permission of Jonathan Cape Publishers,
Hoban/30.10.96.

Cover and text design: John Nedwidek, emdesign
Copy Editor: Bonnie Tilson

Library of Congress Catalog Card Number: 96-71800

ISBN 1-884570-65-8

Printed in the United States of America
99 98 97   5 4 3 2 1

This book is dedicated to Chuck Root, who has shown all who have worked with him how integrity, loyalty, and openness are essential business practices.

THE DISTRIBUTED ENTERPRISE

It was difficult to ascertain the path to my destination, as I was uncertain of my current location. Given this uncertainty, each direction held the promise of both glory and disaster.

• CONTENTS •

CONTENTS

PREFACE

Information technology is a duck. In itself, a duck is a net consumer of resources; it must be contained, requires constant care, becomes less valuable with age, leaves a mess wherever it treads, and is counterproductive until converted into practical application. Caring for ducks requires partners, those who grow the grain, mill the feed, and make the fence wire. Ducks have a mind of their own. They are oblivious to their purpose, and require proactive management if they are to effect a positive result.

Why, in a book about tracking distributed information technology (IT) assets, do I begin with a discussion of ducks? Because as I look at us, those who consume and implement technology, I see that we have become a group of duck aficionados. We have become focused on making faster ducks—whose meat tastes no better, whiter ducks—whose feathers are no softer, bigger ducks—with eggs no larger, and smarter ducks—whose intellect does nothing but make them more difficult to manage.

If technology is to be fully leveraged and is to take its rightful place as a critical thread within the fabric of an organization, we must become duck farmers. This requires that we change our focus from the duck to those consuming the duck, to those supporting our efforts to produce the duck, and to the management of the duck. If we are successful in becoming "duck farmers," our suppliers will become partners, we will assume the mission of the user, and technology will be measured on the rule of mission efficiency.

Becoming a duck farmer requires more than desire and a mission statement; it requires a whole new mind-set. For example, when considering a new implementation of technology for an order entry system, what are the first questions that come to mind? Those focused on the duck find questions such as: What platform and operating system will we use? What is the best way to connect the system? And, what are my resources? While those with a farmer mentality are asking: How much does it cost my users each day they use the old system? Can I modify what is already installed and effect the same results? And, what partners might give me the best ideas?

Because all of this may at first blush seem like esoteric nonsense, I wrote this book around the implementation of a single facet of the "farmer mentality" concept. I regret that I can only address one implementation of this new mind-set. Similar benefits can be found in vendor relations, time-cycle management, user partnering, and many other areas.

Here then is a book written within a broader concept—successfully implemented technology is a single integrated thread within the fabric of the business enterprise. This book—a dramatic and practical example of making the concept a reality.

ACKNOWLEDGMENTS

If you want to know who is truly responsible for any benefit you receive in reading this text, take a moment to skim the names included in the following expression of gratitude.

First, I thank God for all the blessings granted me in allowing this book to be written and published. Primary among those blessings are the scores of individuals who directly and indirectly participated in the intellectual content and creation of this manuscript. As all of these names are too numerous to list, I am forced to thank some contributors as a group. So my first "thank you" goes out to all of those who shared their experiences and trials with me over the past six years. It was their steady progress in managing a base of distributed information technology assets that is the basis for this text. Ladies and gentlemen, your success continues, thank you!

There are also those who offered and sometimes forced their support on me so I might not procrastinate this book out of existence. Thank you Nancy Dunn, Steve Kuekes, Teresa Poppen, and Chuck Root. Without your encouragement and abuse this book would not exist.

My two biggest critics deserve no less thanks as they battled me day after day convincing me that sentences need both a subject and predicate. So thank you Allison David and Tracey Minnich for your relentless editing expertise. I cannot count the number of times you, along with Jim Reece, rescued me from foolishness.

A special thanks to Jae Cody who read this book a dozen times in an effort to give it life and a consistent voice. If this document has a heart, you will find it in rhythm with Jae's pulse.

Finally, I would like to thank my family. Thank you Mandy, Mary, and Rachel, my daughters, for allowing me to use your life experiences as part of this story. Thank you Jennie and Laverne, my dogs, for writing is the loneliest of jobs and you were always there to share the frequent verbal abuse I launched at my word processor. And thank you Judi, my bride, for you are inseparable from any good that comes from me.

So there you have it. The above are those responsible for any merit found in this document. As for the balance, that credit belongs to me, for in spite of my editors' and critics' best efforts, I stand solely responsible for its faults.

INTRODUCTION

Those of you who have seen the movie *The Wizard of Oz* no doubt recognize the title of this book. For those of you who missed the movie, let me briefly set the stage. Dorothy, a young teenager, is swept away by a tornado from the black-and-white world of a Kansas farm to the Technicolor world of the Land of Oz. She looks around and sees colors, landscape, and beings that are beyond her imagination, not to mention her experience, and dryly exclaims to her dog, "Gee, Toto, we're not in Kansas anymore." And so, with this same feeling, I began my precarious journey into the world of managing distributed information technology (IT) resources.

This journey, like Dorothy's, was quite unintentional. As chief executive officer of a software development company, I set out six years ago to deliver a superior electronic software distribution solution. This product, in theory, allowed organizations to electronically distribute new versions of software to distributed desktops and servers (i.e., the distributed enterprise) in an unattended fashion. Thanks to the efforts of some supremely talented individuals, this endeavor succeeded in that several hundred Fortune 500-sized organizations use this product for its intended purpose. This book, however, is not about the success of this product—or for that matter, any product. This book is about the bumps that hundreds of business managers and IT professionals, including myself, encountered as we attempted to embrace an IT enterprise that was geographically dispersed, underfunded, overcommitted, and managed by an anarchy of end users whose vision of the enterprise stopped at their own desktops.

In reality, this book was conceived the first time I asked a very competent Fortune 500 chief information officer, "So what does your distributed enterprise look like?" His answer—and the collective answer I would hear hundreds of times over the next six years—was, "Well, plus or minus 30 percent, I don't have a clue."

His answer did not reflect a lack of competence, but rather the recognition that the enterprise had evolved from both the top down and the bottom up, via local projects and corporate projects, and with a liberal number of end-user authorized and unauthorized changes to a corporate standard that is unenforced by those demanding perfection. Here is the confusing landscape of our electronic Oz.

Yet within this confusion there were those who refused to wander aimlessly. Admittedly, their compass was no better than the rest, but they kept an accurate map of where they had been and were kind enough to share the location of the mile markers they established as part of their journey through the world of managing distributed IT assets. This book is a summary of those mile markers. They allow us to establish our relative position in the journey of managing our distributed IT assets, and they guide us in the general direction of the next known point in our journey.

Two final thoughts. First, if you are looking for an overly serious, statistically-based, analytical study of IT asset management, then this book will make a nice coaster for your coffee mug. If on the other hand, you are looking for a dozen or two practical necessities for effectively managing and tracking your distributed IT asset base, then you will have to find another place for your mug. And second, although believing IT asset tracking is critical to the survival of most organizations, I do not rank the topic up there with world hunger or political freedom. Accordingly, I have kept the tone of the book on the light side. This tone is in no way meant to demean the wisdom and experience that has been entrusted to me; it is merely my attempt to construct this book as a conversation between two friends.

Best of luck in Oz...

A JOURNEY THROUGH
OZ

CHAPTER 1
• SIMPLE •

Me: *(Saying good-bye to my daughter, as I dropped her off at college at the outset of her freshman year)* I feel like I should say something profound.

Amanda (my daughter): This is pretty confusing; I could use "profound" right now.

Me: The best advice I can give you in your new journey is for you to aspire to simple things, for simplicity and greatness are frequent companions. When you find yourself following a path of increasing complexity, stop!—for you are headed toward diminishing returns.

Amanda: Just as simple as getting good grades, right?

Me: Oh no, good grades are complex. They depend on so many factors: the course material, the professor, your aptitude, and study materials. There's nothing simple about good grades.

Amanda: Then what is simple?

Me: The principles in the Bible, the Spartan's stand at Thermopylae, the calling heard by Martin Luther, and the building of the Hoover Dam—at the heart of each of these is simplicity.

Amanda: You mean focused conviction. How about a commitment to do the very best I can?

Me: You see how simple it is? Amanda, I believe you shall touch greatness.

Amanda has excelled in college. She will graduate a year early with a double major in English and Spanish. She would tell you the trick to her success was simple: just do the best you can on every homework assignment, every paper, every quiz, every test, and in every class session. Of course she would also add that simple does not necessarily mean easy.

Amanda's learned trick is something that we, in the pursuit of excellence within our organizations, often forget. The greatest progress is made via commitment to simple understandings. I include this bit of philosophy at the beginning of this book as I fear that in my zeal to express the power of managing distributed information technology (IT) resources, I will shroud the topic in complexity. There is nothing complex about the underlying principle of this book. If an organization is going to succeed and survive in the competitive global economy, it must proactively manage its distributed IT resources.

This theorem can be expressed in the form of an equation:

GIVEN
employees = product, creativity, and survival

THEREFORE
employees = our most valued asset

GIVEN
employee productivity = access to a stable base of
distributed IT assets

THEREFORE
proactive management of distributed IT assets = employee
productivity and survival of the organization

This relationship between an employee and technology is of increasing interest to successful management teams. Employees and their desktops are now being viewed as a single unit of productivity (i.e., knowledge unit) as both the employee and the desktop are ineffective without the other. The management of these resources around the knowledge unit concept is simple, yet it offers an extraordinary opportunity to those who focus on its potential.

Forward-thinking industry leaders, including chief information officers (CIOs), chief financial officers (CFOs), purchasing executives, senior general managers, and security and legal professionals, are aggressively pursuing the productivity gains that can be realized via the processes outlined in this book. These gains are expressed in many terms, including improved employee productivity, cost savings, asset leveraging, and expense deferrals; but ultimately, these gains track back to how much additional product we can generate per employee asset. In corporate terms, this is translated into cents per share, return on assets, return on investment, or a host of other measurements. In the end, it is simply the victorious global competitor looking at the vanquished, saying, "My guy can make more than your guy."

What kind of productivity gains can you expect to attain by proactively managing your distributed client/server enterprise assets? To answer this you must estimate how much time average end users spend fighting with the technology on their desktops. How many hours per week is the same average user distracted by the appeal of the Internet's World Wide Web? How much employee productivity is siphoned off by counterproductive upgrades, overpayment to hardware and software suppliers, and theft? The calculation of improved productivity is certainly organization dependent; but responses from knowledgeable executives typically range from 5 to 25 percent.

And so we return to the concept of simplicity. Organizations regularly implement elaborate and complex schemes in an effort to improve the bottom line (e.g., productivity enhancement programs that often net improvement by only tenths of a percentage point). Examples of such activity include whole classes of assets being enveloped in a convoluted lease program to marginally improve financial reports, companies purchasing their own satellite links in an effort to shave a few points off their communications expense, and elaborate self-insurance programs being implemented to modestly reduce the cost of employee benefits. These complex schemes do yield results. However, greater results can be obtained from this simple concept: We need to know what distributed IT assets we have, and we need to proactively manage those assets.

Here, in this simple concept, is the opportunity to realize huge efficiencies. But as Amanda would tell you, simple is not always easy. Putting a man on the moon was driven by man's simple desire to touch the soil of another world. The insurmountable, tedious, complex, and daunting details of this effort were conquered only when viewed through the optics of the dream.

Fortunately, the successful implementation of a solution that allows you to track distributed assets is not a complex task. Such a system (i.e., an asset tracking solution) gives you an understanding of what your assets look like today, as well as the speed and direction of their change. If this book attains its stated purpose, it will provide managers of various disciplines with a blueprint of a solution that delivers the benefits of effective enterprise asset tracking. There will, however, still be challenges along the way, as those responsible for the mission deal with gross World Wide Web abuse, unauthorized software, missing equipment, and disgruntled vendors who have been denied undeserved margins. These challenges and more await those who proactively manage their distributed IT assets. Awaiting too, however, are the disproportionate rewards of embracing the simplicity of productivity.

Here, in these pages, is your map of Oz. The Wizard can be found in the Emerald City...the Yellow Brick Road in chapters 2 through 11. Enjoy the journey.

CHAPTER 2

• BORING BUT NECESSARY •

Publisher: You wrote a book on what?

Me: Managing distributed information technology (IT) resources.

Publisher: The what?

Me: You know, a vast network of clients and servers.

Publisher: Who's going to read this book?

Me: People whose professional lives depend on this fragile network of resources.

Publisher: Sorry, we're only going with material that has sex, violence, or the World Wide Web as a theme.

Me: Well, I might be able to work the Web in…

Publisher: Juice it up and shoot me a copy.

As the above conversation highlights, there is no public outcry for a book on managing distributed IT resources. And the reason is simple—most managers have not been exposed to the broad benefits of proactively managing the distributed enterprise. However, once the benefits are understood, even the most detached manager discovers a curiosity for the topic.

It is at this point that the primary obstacle in generating interest is encountered: How do you entertain a spirited dialog on a topic without a common understanding, and how do you gain a common understanding without making an investment in learning the language (terms) of the studied topic? The remainder of this chapter is devoted to establishing a common vocabulary of terms and an understanding of the audience that will benefit from acquiring this knowledge. So then, this is the requisite dry chapter, aptly named "Boring But Necessary." But stick with it, for although it may be boring, it will return big dividends as you move through the more stimulating chapters.

AUDIENCE

As the business benefits of better managing distributed IT assets far outweigh the technical benefits, this book is written at a high level, focusing on business operations. With the exception of chapter 10, all chapters use a minimum of technical jargon and the management of distributed IT assets is approached from a business perspective. Even with this business emphasis, you will find that a high-level discussion of technological concepts is frequently part of a topic. This is necessary because often the specific application of a technology is directly responsible for the associated business benefits. It would be an injustice to you not to tie the two together. Even with the aforementioned confession, this book primarily targets senior managers and executives of large organizations across all industries who are concerned with overall IT resource productivity and utilization. In particular, top executives in the areas of information technology, purchasing, finance, legal, operations, help desk, corporate security, and general management will find it especially informative.

Senior technologists and middle managers with a broad interest in business, and who view technology as a means to attaining business objectives, will find this book equally informative. In many cases, these are the individuals who have brought to light many of the concepts contained in this book. And it is this group, whose members value technology for its vast business utility, that shall find themselves the senior managers of the future.

SCOPE OF DISCUSSION

For most technology consumers, interest in distributed IT resources stops at their own desktops. And for the most part, those consumers who do care avoid thinking about IT resources because the issue is so complex. For those interested and committed few, the process of managing a distributed enterprise of IT assets begins with trying to define the topic. Desktops, servers, bridges, routers, LANs, WANs, protocols, bandwidth, T1 lines, switches, downstream, upstream…these are just a few of the items that make up the distributed IT enterprise. Complicating matters further, each item that makes up this distributed pool of resources has its own set of terms and a self-important view of its role in the enterprise. How then, in a book this size, can one expect to convey any meaningful insight into managing these distributed IT assets? By cheating!

I have chosen to focus on the end point (the end-user desktops and servers) of the distributed enterprise. Although some may view this approach as cheating, in reality it is the quintessential element to managing distributed IT assets. Since the end point is where services are delivered, it is here that organizations can realize the greatest productivity gains. And it is here that the winners are separated from the losers in the race for superior productivity and enhanced bottom lines.

The questions surrounding these end-point assets are basic. What desktops and servers do you have? Where are they located? How are they configured? What is the direction and pace with which they are changing? If you cannot answer these questions, then no matter how well your enterprise is bridged, and no matter how tightly integrated your applications are, you will in the end fail, for it is these desktops and servers that stand between the enterprise and the end user, and between the end user and productivity. Accordingly, this book explores the techniques and opportunities for managing the end point of the distributed IT asset base.

CONCEPTS AND TERMS

The following is a list of concepts and terms that are frequently used in this text.

CLIENTS AND SERVERS

Within the context of this book, clients are the end-user desktops that make up the enterprise. These desktops include the processing units, monitors, a complement of communications hardware and software, operating system software, shrink-wrap (vendor supplied) software, in-house developed software, and attached devices such as a CD-ROM. Servers include the same complement of items as the clients, plus the additional hardware and software that allow them to provide shared services to the client/end-user desktops.

DISTRIBUTED ENTERPRISE
(DISTRIBUTED IT ASSETS)

A distributed enterprise is an amalgamation of client and server resources that support the business objectives of the organization. These resources can be actively connected (networked), passively connected (dial-in via a modem), or logically connected (via their utility to the business objectives).

COMMUNICATIONS INFRASTRUCTURE
(NETWORK)

The communications infrastructure includes the wires, communications lines, protocols, bridges, routers, and network management services that maintain the actively and passively connected distributed enterprise. Only a small portion of this book deals with the communications infrastructure, and then only as it relates to desktop and server productivity.

POINTS OF CHANGE

Points of change are the changes taking place to the client and server platforms. Since it is not possible to include an explanation of all changes that may affect the enterprise, a list of change sources is included. As this entire text is based on the tracking and management of changes to the distributed IT enterprise, below are some of the sources of change as they relate to this text.

- End-user modifications include changes to the operating system configuration, the authorized or unauthorized addition or removal of hardware components or applications, and modifications to applications and services delivered by "corporate."

- Server administrator modifications include the same changes covered under end-user modifications, plus hardware, software, and communications modifications that are unique to the server platform.

- Enterprise-directed modifications include "corporate" changes made to the desktops and servers via electronic software distribution, manually distributed media, or communications reconfigurations.

- Business-directed modifications are a result of changes to business operations. A comprehensive summary of these types of changes is too extensive to list; however, it is important to note that even a seemingly insignificant business-directed modification can have a profound impact on the distributed IT enterprise. Consider, for example, the "cascade effect" of hiring a new employee into a department. In many cases, the new desktop purchased as part of that hire does not go to the new employee, but to the most-senior member of the department. This senior employee, in turn, cascades the old system to the next most-senior member of the department. It is easy to see how the hiring of a single employee can end up changing several dozen desktops.

SETTING THE STAGE

DISTRIBUTED IT RESOURCE MANAGEMENT

The "state of the art" in managing distributed IT assets is presently centered on the ability to collect current IT asset information more frequently and with less effort. Although this is a desirable objective, there is a more advanced generation of solutions which, if understood, can provide business benefits far beyond a timely inventory. The remainder of this chapter contrasts the current "state of the art," an institutional perspective, and a more "visionary" solution for managing the distributed IT asset base.

TRADITIONAL VIEW

Managing a distributed IT asset base is generally synonymous with maintaining an accurate inventory of the desktops and servers. This process is typically accomplished via some combination of electronic discovery and a large group of temporary employees or contractors who gather and consolidate the discovered information on an annual basis. The cost of gathering this information, as detailed in a later chapter, is substantial. These high financial costs, along with the disruption that an inventory causes to end-user productivity, make anything other than annual inventories impractical.

INSTITUTIONAL VIEW

This "once-a-year view" of the distributed IT enterprise, although valuable, is of limited utility. This is why industry experts are presently promoting a new class of asset management software that uses an organization's network to collect and consolidate desktop and server profiles. This new paradigm allows the distributed IT enterprise to be inventoried more frequently and with less end-user disruption. Those advocating this new asset inventory process include it as a peer in an architecture of enterprise management solutions. This architecture is illustrated below:

ENTERPRISE MANAGEMENT			
ASSET MANAGEMENT (INVENTORY) SYSTEMS	APPLICATION CHANGE MANAGEMENT	HELP DESK SYSTEMS	AUTOMATED PURCHASING SYSTEMS
SYSTEMS MANAGEMENT TOOLS	CONFIGURATION CHANGE MANAGEMENT	APPLICATION MANAGEMENT TOOLS	SOFTWARE DISTRIBUTION
ENTERPRISE CHANGE MANAGEMENT	NETWORK MANAGEMENT TOOLS	FIXED ASSET SYSTEMS	OTHERS...

This paradigm is a giant leap forward over traditional methods of managing the distributed IT enterprise because it can provide views of the enterprise on a more frequent basis, with minimal end-user disruption. By having a peer-level facility that provides more current desktop and server information, another layer of depth is added to the management of the enterprise.

A NEW VISION

Although I agree with those calling for more frequent and less labor-intensive views of the enterprise, this is only one step toward effective management of the distributed IT assets.

Arguably, a system that gathers and reports information on the desktop and server complex can be categorized not as a peer, but as an infrastructure for the management of the enterprise. By joining and sharing distributed IT asset information in an open repository, a new infrastructure is created. This infrastructure enables all enterprise management facilities to extend their utility. Further, these management tools can add their unique view of the distributed IT assets to the repository, thereby further enriching each management tool's utility. A diagram highlighting the differences between the institutional view and a new vision for an IT asset repository is illustrated below:

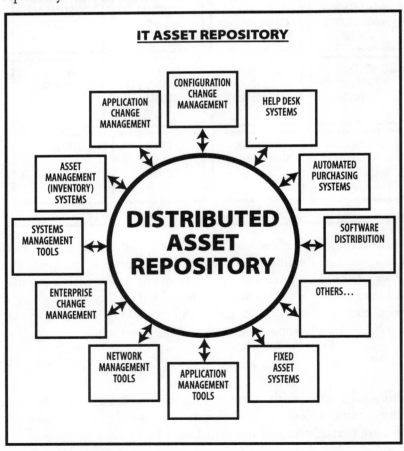

This diagram highlights the two-way communication between the various enterprise tools. For example, the open repository gives the help desk system access to the latest configuration information for a user who is having problems, and it enables a problem history of each individual desktop and server to be added to the repository. The result of this exchange is improved enterprise visibility for all enterprise management functions.

The free flow of information depicted in the diagram is a future goal for many organizations. However, the tools and asset tracking systems that enable such exchanges are available today.

With such an infrastructure in place, applications, tools, and managers can discover the current state of any client or server in the enterprise and how it relates to other enterprise functions. This, however, is only the first step in realizing the full power of the asset repository. By keeping multiple images of each distributed asset configuration over time, regression and sensitivity analyses can be performed on the distributed asset base, thereby extending its utility from an operations tool to a tracking and planning device.

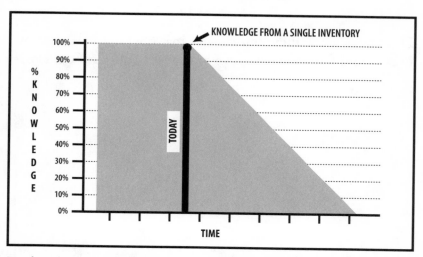

In the above graph, the gray area represents the knowledge base that is available from a system that maintains multiple images of the distributed IT assets over time, while the black line represents the knowledge captured from a current single inventory. The graph highlights the fact that by having a historical base of knowledge, you can gain visibility into the future. This topic is covered in greater detail in later chapters.

Beyond this is the opportunity to provide front-ends to the repository that analyze, track, and report on activities that would otherwise go unnoticed by even the most diligent enterprise staff. As later chapters will illustrate, joining expertise, technology, and a historical base of knowledge allows for the conversion of raw data into valuable insights.

These capabilities are available today to those who understand the benefits of reaching beyond the concept of a simple inventory. Awaiting too are the false starts and dead ends that confront the uninformed. With this in mind, the balance of this book explores the possibilities and pitfalls of creating and leveraging a distributed asset repository.

SUMMARY

Definitions are nothing but hangers that hold our ideas, lest our intellections find themselves in a heap at the bottom of our closet.

CHAPTER 3
• COMPARED TO WHAT? •

Me: How did the calculus exam go?

Mary (my daughter): Great!

Me: What does great mean?

Mary: Upper 2 percent of my class!

Me: What was the class average?

Mary: Thirty-one percent.

Me: And your grade?

Mary: Thirty-eight percent.

Me: Then you failed?

Mary: Yes, but it was a hard test.

This is a fair approximation of a conversation I had with my oldest daughter several years ago. Mary, who is really a very good student, failed to give me the comparative information necessary for me to make an informed assessment of her performance. At Mary's insistence, and in the spirit of full disclosure, the teacher graded on a curve, and Mary got a "D" for her efforts. All of this appears to speak to parenting; however, it holds an equally profound lesson for managing distributed IT assets.

The connection to my daughter's grades can best be illustrated through example. For the purposes of this exercise, assume you have before you a complete audit of all software, hardware, and peripherals that comprise your distributed client/server enterprise. This information is displayed or printed in a manner that allows you to view each machine and its associated assets as a unit, and is cross-tabulated to give you an item count for each type of asset. Further, assume this information was gathered at the exact same instant and is accurate plus or minus 1 percent. No doubt, for most managers this would be a giant step forward in the control of their distributed asset base. In fact, it is nearly a perfect inventory! Well...sounds like we solved this problem; let's get a cold beer and call it a day.

As tempting as that might be, there is a substantial base of evidence that suggests managers are lacking the most critical components of an asset tracking system. Notice the distinction between asset inventory and asset tracking. This distinction results from distributed IT assets having unique qualities that traditional assets (e.g., cars, desks, and machine tools) lack.

Distributed IT assets are constantly undergoing an evolutionary process as software, storage, memory, applications, connectivity, and the computer itself are upgraded, modified, or replaced. Complicating this evolution is the number of sources of change involved, including corporate management information systems (MIS), server administrators, end users, application vendors, and departmental management. In an effort to make sense out of this perpetual migration, forward-thinking professionals use "comparative anchors" to assist in making this evolution both manageable and meaningful.

A comparative anchor is nothing more than a figurative stationary point to which we can tie the ever-evolving asset. In linking an evolving asset to a stationary point, we have the ability to establish the asset's actual position, as well as its relative position to other events and assets that have a convergence of interest.

There are numerous comparative anchors that are indispensable in the management of the enterprise. In the interest of being brief, and since my editor told me 150 pages tops, I have highlighted the anchors that have the broadest applicability to a general audience. Each of these anchors is valuable and can be indispensable in the management of the enterprise. As you study this short list of comparative anchors, keep in mind that the final anchor, "Your Comparative Anchor," offers the greatest potential return on investment (ROI). It is this anchor that allows the assets to be associated with the unique properties of your business operations.

SURVEY OF ANCHORS

TIME COMPARATIVE ANCHOR

The grandest of all comparative anchors is time. Because assets are forever changing and evolving, time becomes the most informative element in the tracking of distributed IT assets. The case studies presented in later chapters highlight the power of a time-based analysis. However, for now, consider the following examples: A CFO can view the value of the IT assets as of a specific date. A help desk analyst can view a snapshot (i.e., a stored inventory for a particular moment in time) of a workstation before and after an end-user problem occurs. A purchasing executive can determine a license count for a specific software application as of a given point in time. Each of these inventories becomes meaningful as a result of being "time anchored."

TRENDS COMPARATIVE ANCHOR

Russell Hoban wrote in *The Lion of Boaz-Jachin*, "If the past cannot teach the present and the father cannot teach the son, then history need not have bothered to go on, and the world has wasted a great deal of time." If we, as senior managers and executives, are to avoid wasting time in the management of the IT asset base, then we must regard and use trending as one of our primary weapons.   Actually, trending is a by-product of the Time Comparative Anchor in that it acts as a type of radar. Trending reports on the movement, speed, and direction of the changing distributed IT asset base. This radar is nothing more than plotting the same asset point over multiple time periods and ascertaining its rate of change and future direction.

Consider a CFO who has the ability to predict the desktop turnover rate and, thus, improve overall cash management. Or, consider an IT executive who can accurately predict a usage trend for a particular software application before beginning negotiations with the application vendor. How about a purchasing executive who, by using trend analysis, can determine when users will run out of disk space, allowing for favorable volume purchasing decisions? The Trends Comparative Anchor allows us to use the past and present to better forecast the future.

PHANTOM COMPARATIVE ANCHOR

Some of the most powerful comparative anchors are neither other assets nor time. These Phantom Comparative Anchors are tags, knowledge, or some type of organization identifier that is associated with the asset. In our "nearly perfect" inventory scenario presented earlier, we had all the "physical information" about our distributed IT asset base; however, the usefulness of this information, without Phantom Comparative Anchors, is limited. Consider the improved utility of this same data if these physical assets are associated with a specific employee, phone number, address, building, department, job title, manager, general ledger account, or priority code. None of these Phantom Comparative Anchors has value in themselves. But, when Phantom Comparative Anchors are combined with the inventory data and historical snapshots, they become powerful tools in managing not just the enterprise, but the entire business process.

My favorite quote regarding the value of Phantom Comparative Anchors comes from an MIS director who was faced with the rather mundane task of upgrading the software in the finance department. He exclaimed, "I can track every desktop down to a specific network address. I get an update on every desktop configuration twice a year, and I know the names and locations of every employee in this company.... But tell you which desktops and servers belong to the finance department? Forget it!" Phantom Comparative Anchors give dimension to an otherwise flat base of asset information.

NULL COMPARATIVE ANCHOR

I read in Will Durant's *The Story of Civilization* that the ancient Egyptians, the most advanced culture of their day, ceased progressing because they never developed the mathematical concept of "zero." The Egyptians, in missing zero, lost sustained greatness. Within this irony we discover the value of the Null Comparative Anchor. Sometimes the most valuable information is in knowing something isn't there.

Consider the impact of a business unit manager being alerted that a particular group of workstations is missing the current version of a critical rate table. Or consider the productivity benefits of having a listing of all workstations and servers that do not have the "corporate standard configuration."

Even more interesting results can be attained by combining Time Comparative Anchors with Null Comparative Anchors. By comparing the current snapshot of the desktops with the next most recent snapshot of the same desktops, we can discover which machines have less main memory from one period to the next, less online storage, a missing CD-ROM, etc. At times, the value of knowing what you don't have is greater than the value of counting your possessions.

REFLECTIVE COMPARATIVE ANCHOR

One of my favorite quotes concerning knowledge comes from Denis Diderot, the French philosopher who said, "There are three principal means of acquiring knowledge available to us: observation of nature, reflection, and experimentation. Observation collects facts; reflection combines them; experimentation verifies the result of that combination." The Reflective Comparative Anchor addresses the combination of facts. By reflecting static information off of other bases of knowledge, we gain insight. For example, to know that the number of WordPerfect installations is declining across the enterprise is knowledge; to know that 100 percent of high-end users (knowledge workers) run WordPerfect is insight. There is an infinite number of examples of how combining information sets can lead to profound insight; several case studies are included in chapters 3, 4, 5, 6, and 9 that highlight the value of such insights.

YOUR COMPARATIVE ANCHOR(S)

One of my most valued customers is a large and very successful insurance company. I have no doubt that this customer, although wholeheartedly endorsing the value of the aforementioned anchors, would identify this final anchor as the most important means of comparison. The reason for elevating the priority of this anchor is based on the leverage a business-specific anchor can provide to the business enterprise.

This insurance company considers its 4,000 independent agents to be a significant part of both the company's business and its IT enterprise. Accordingly, the company supplies its agents with a wealth of software customized to each individual agent. Within this customization is information (making up Your Comparative Anchor) on the type of policies the agent writes, the agent's name, address, performance history, etc. Part of this customer's newly installed asset tracking system allows it to gather the agent information (from the installed customized software) as part of the desktop inventory. By extracting this business information from the supplied software, and tying it to the IT resources (the agents' desktops) that support the mission-critical application, the insurance company is able to provide a superior level of customized support to its agent population. The joining of information resources and business knowledge allows the company to improve the productivity of its agents' policy-writing efforts, and anticipate its agents' technology needs and problems. There is no line between the business enterprise and the technology enterprise; each supports the other by providing insight and productivity gains that are mutually beneficial.

SUMMARY

If you want to know what you have, count it; if you want to know what is happening to it, compare it!

CASE STUDY 1
NOW YOU SEE IT, NOW YOU DON'T

PROLOGUE

XYZ is a large insurance company with forty major field offices in eleven countries. XYZ has a distributed enterprise model that allows for some level of autonomy and buying authority within each geographic location, business unit, and functional department. The responsibility for managing and supporting the distributed enterprise falls under the information technology group, which is headed by a CIO.

ENTERPRISE DEFINITION

XYZ's distributed enterprise includes approximately 30,000 desktops, which are supported by 2,700 servers. Three different server platforms and four desktop platforms are supported. The enterprise is geographically dispersed with large groups of users in Chicago, London, Boston, and San Francisco.

THE SITUATION/PROBLEM

The company recently developed, and plans to put into production within thirty days, a major financial consolidation system that involves all of the distributed desktops within the finance department. During a trip to several of the major field locations to check on the progress of the implementation, the CIO requests a demonstration of the new system. In Chicago, the field agent giving the demonstration encounters an "out-of-main-memory condition" that prohibits the completion of the demonstration. A quick analysis indicates the affected system does not have the required complement of memory to run the application, even though all systems were supposed to have been upgraded to the requisite configuration thirty days earlier. The CIO makes a note of the agent's name and network address and continues his tour.

THE FIRST STEP

Knowing that all 2,900 Chicago desktops targeted to support the new financial consolidation system were scheduled for a memory upgrade to be completed thirty days ago, the CIO queries the asset tracking system to determine which of these do not have the proper memory configuration. The latest snapshot of the systems in question shows that 280 of the 2,900 systems do not have the required sixteen megabytes (MB) of main memory. The CIO runs a report identifying the desktops requiring a memory upgrade to support the new application and an effort begins to upgrade the deficient systems.

Here we see the power of having an up-to-date inventory of the distributed enterprise. The deficient desktops scheduled to go into production in less than thirty days are identified before they fail, and remedial action is taken. Even if the CIO had not noticed the glitch, standard procedures can enforce a final check of all targeted systems before the new software is deployed. All of this speaks to the power of having a current inventory, but much more can be learned as the CIO begins to leverage the historical information available from the asset tracking system.

TRACKING DOWN A PROBLEM

With a plan in place to correct the memory deficiency, the CIO turns his attention to the more strategic question: Which of the 2,900 Chicago desktops targeted for the memory upgrade were actually upgraded to the prerequisite configuration thirty days ago as planned? To his surprise, all 2,900 desktops reported having memory upgraded for the new financial consolidation system by the designated date. A specific check of the system that failed during the demonstration shows that thirty days earlier it too reported a full memory complement.

Somewhat perplexed by these asset changes, the CIO runs an enterprise-wide Suspicious Activity Analysis. There are three sections to this analysis, each providing its own insight into the source of the problem. *Note: Although such an analysis would ideally appear on a single page, for formatting purposes, this book presents them in a series.*

SUSPICIOUS ACTIVITY ANALYSIS

SUSPICIOUS ACTIVITY ANALYSIS — SUMMARY

The first section of this analysis provides a framework for understanding the other sections of the report.

SUMMARY

An analysis of the 30,114 desktops tracked during the period ending 3/15 reveals 2,264 suspicious activities. Of these, 977 are desktops that failed to report within 7 days of their scheduled inventories, 578 show a decline in the number of hard disks, 690 show a decline in memory, and 19 are missing a CD-ROM.

The total number of suspicious activities is 70 percent greater than the previous month.

SUSPICIOUS ACTIVITY ANALYSIS — DEPARTMENTAL BREAKDOWN

The second section of this report takes the Summary and breaks it down by functional business units.

The insight derived from the table on the next page begins with the far right column, "% of enterprise." This information provides XYZ's CIO with a frame of reference when examining the various departmental counts (four center columns, shaded) of suspicious activity. The CIO notices in the first row that finance has 23 percent of all enterprise desktops, but appears to have a disproportionate number of desktops (540) reporting a decrease in main memory.

DEPARTMENT	NOT REPORTING	DECLINE IN MEMORY	DECLINE IN HARD DISKS	MISSING CD-ROMs	% OF ENTERPRISE
FINANCE	118	540	136	0	23%
MARKETING	128	80	129	0	16%
SALES	232	46	99	0	27%
ACTUARIAL	410	21	109	19	16%
OTHER	89	3	105	0	18%
TOTAL	977	690	578	19	100%

SUSPICIOUS ACTIVITY ANALYSIS — SNAPSHOTS OVER TIME

The third section of the analysis enriches each element by presenting it in a historical context and graphically displaying its speed and direction (trend).

The information provided in the Departmental Breakdown, although significant, does not tell a complete story. To fully comprehend the significance of the numbers in the table, they must be examined within the context of time. To assist in this examination, the analysis includes a trend analysis for each element. Each of these analyses plots a specific type of suspicious activity over time. A table of numerical values represented in the charts is summarized below:

	1/1	1/15	2/1	2/15	3/1	3/15
NOT REPORTING	676	600	519	630	625	977
DECLINE IN MEMORY	180	585	156	141	163	690
DECLINE IN HARD DISKS	218	355	410	489	535	578
MISSING CD-ROMs	0	0	1	3	8	19

DESKTOPS NOT REPORTING

The following graph plots the number of desktops not reporting (i.e., updating the repository with a new snapshot of the desktop) on the scheduled date for the past six snapshot periods. Note: In this case the snapshots were taken every two weeks.

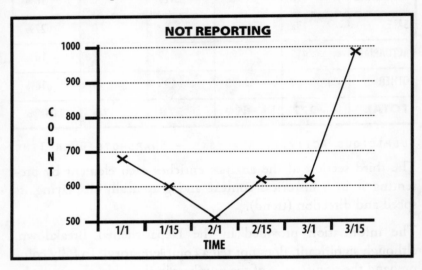

When examining the Desktops Not Reporting graph, the CIO notices an unusual spike not apparent when reviewing the finance department on the Departmental Breakdown. In referring back to the breakdown table, he discovers the problem is centered in the actuarial department (with 410 desktops not reporting), which causes him to initiate an investigation.

DECLINE IN MEMORY

Temporarily setting aside the issue of Desktops Not Reporting, the CIO turns to the next trend analysis, Decline in Memory. Here, there is a strong indication that some form of undesirable activity is linked to the failed software demonstration in Chicago.

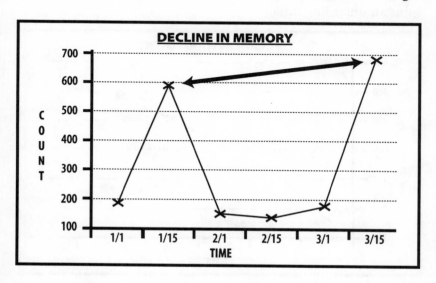

In examining the above graph, the CIO notices spikes in main memory decline for the snapshot periods of 1/15 and 3/15 (arrows) indicating there may be some outside element involved. The CIO makes a copy of the Suspicious Activity Analysis and sends it, along with a detailed listing of affected users, departments, and locations, to corporate security.

DECLINE IN HARD DISKS

When looking at the Departmental Breakdown, the "Decline in Hard Disks" column does not show any unusual distribution between departments and, therefore, receives little of the CIO's attention. In examining this element over time, however, the CIO gains an unsettling insight.

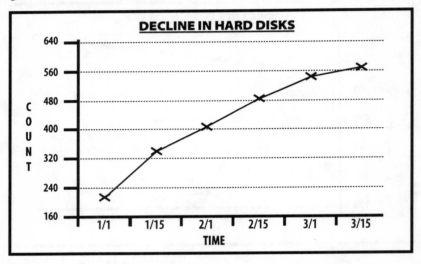

According to the above graph, the number of desktops experiencing a decrease in hard disk capacity has nearly tripled over the past six snapshot periods. This trend and the supporting details are also sent to corporate security for investigation.

MISSING CD-ROMs

The last element in the analysis, Missing CD-ROMs, also has no relevance to the initial investigation, as the finance department reported no occurrence of this type of suspicious activity. However, the CIO discovers an undesirable upward trend in missing CD-ROMs for the corporation overall. With a look back at the Departmental Breakdown, he realizes that this trend can be tied back to the actuarial department.

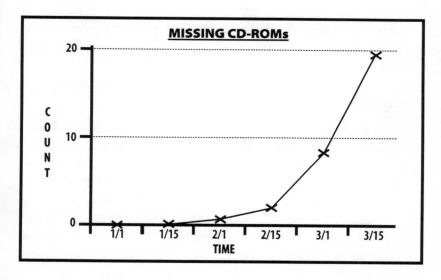

Because of the small numbers involved (nineteen missing CD-ROMs on 3/15), and because of a close working relationship, the CIO places a call to the vice president in charge of the actuarial department. As a result, the vice president requests a report detailing the users involved; he then initiates an informal investigation.

Epilogue

An epilogue is included in this hypothetical case study to highlight some of the discoveries that MIS professionals have shared with me in the management of their distributed enterprise.

As a result of the CIO's investigation of the anomalies highlighted in the Suspicious Activity Analysis, it is learned that:

• The two spikes in Decline in Memory coincide with the use of a specific contractor hired to perform data entry during off hours. In both cases, this contractor was employed in the finance department during the time period when main memory chips were removed from the desktops. The various purchasing agencies are notified, and the vendor is suspended pending further investigation.

• The Decline in Hard Disks proves to be a broader problem. Corporate security, by tracking a serial number in a lower capacity drive, discovers that a small but increasing percentage of employees have been removing the small-capacity drives from their personal home systems and swapping them with the larger-capacity drives on their office desktops. These employees are "counseled," and corporate security initiates a campaign to inform all employees that such activity will be closely monitored in the future.

• The Missing CD-ROM investigation proves to be less dramatic. Some employees in the actuarial department, while working on a large project with a tight deadline, were permitted to remove their external CD-ROM drive and use it at home over the weekend. The snapshot, which was taken early Monday morning, detected those drives that had not yet been reconnected. The policy that allows employees, in an effort to meet corporate deadlines, to take equipment home over the weekend also explains the large number of Desktops Not Reporting. XYZ institutes a formal sign-out policy that enables the tracking of equipment that leaves the premises.

FROM THEORY TO APPLICATION

This case study highlights the utility of the seemingly academic concepts covered at the beginning of this chapter. The Time Comparative Anchor is necessary to establish that the upgrades had been performed on schedule and that the memory deficient desktops were more than just an oversight. The Trends Comparative Anchor allows the CIO to quantify the nature and severity of the problem. The Phantom Comparative Anchor permits the association of assets to departments and users. The Null Comparative Anchor is the basis for the entire analysis in that it highlights missing elements. And finally, the Reflective Comparative Anchor not only enables a comparison between departments, but also allows the CIO to compare departmental counts against their percentage representation within the enterprise.

• WHO NEEDS IT ANYWAY? •

Me: Excuse me, I heard that the heavy snow has the ramp to the tunnel blocked. Can you tell me another route to Logan Airport?

Hotel Clerk: Here, I have a map. Let me show you. *(Clerk gives me a map.)*

Me: *(After driving eight miles in three hours only to find the airport closed)* I need a room—the airport is closed until tomorrow.

Hotel Clerk: Yeah, I thought it was funny that you were in such a hurry to get there.... Sorry, we're all booked up.

Me: You mean when you gave me directions, you knew the airport was closed?

Hotel Clerk: Sure did.

Me: WHY DIDN'T YOU TELL ME?

Hotel Clerk: It didn't seem important to you.

Here is an experience that taught me three valuable lessons. First, not all hotel clerks are working to fund an education in rocket science. Second, never, never, never give up a hotel room in a snowstorm. Third, sometimes we, and others, do not know what we need. Now, although I am tempted to write this chapter on the second of these lessons—since spending the night at the airport trying to sleep in a phone booth cubicle provides a world of instruction—I have elected to focus on the third.

Oftentimes in our intimate understanding of a topic, we fail to see the utility of our knowledge beyond the scope of our own needs. IT professionals and other decision makers who undertake the task of actively tracking the distributed enterprise are consistently surprised by the broad application of the information and analysis that results from even the most basic asset tracking system. Clearly, if all the utility of an asset tracking system were known in advance of their efforts, IT professionals would have designed a more flexible and forward-thinking solution. The remainder of this chapter describes the application of asset tracking data across departmental boundaries. It is in considering these "milestones of utility" that we have the best opportunity to build a tracking solution that tells the rest of the world, "By the way, did you know the airport is closed until tomorrow morning?"

The following presents a brief survey of the utility of asset tracking across seven business units. It is not intended to be an exhaustive list of either functionality or scope. I chose these departments and these examples as a means of opening up the universe, not defining the city limits. And if you ask yourself as you read this, "Why didn't he include this?" or "How could he omit a discussion of that?" then I have accomplished my task, as you have already begun to expand the universe of utility provided by an asset tracking solution.

FINANCE

When we first think of asset tracking within the context of the finance department, we think of a year-end physical inventory. There are many studies of how much it costs to inventory distributed IT assets, ranging from $30 per seat to $250 per seat. Clearly, some form of automated inventory would go a long way toward paying for an asset tracking system. There is, however, a broader set of questions we must consider if we are to view asset tracking from a financial perspective, including some form of automated reconciliation with the existing fixed-asset accounting system. Any links or automated functions that enable the tracking system to match and report variances between what it finds and what is being carried on the books can, over time, improve both the accuracy of what is reported and the bottom line.

Consider the reconciliation of the fixed-asset accounting system with the current information reported by the asset tracking system. A single line from such a report might disclose that the fixed-asset accounting system lists 3,814 Intel 386-class machines in service, while the tracking system found only 114 such machines attached to the network! This brings to mind a long list of questions, including: Where are the other 3,700 machines? How do we account for the remaining useful life of the 3,700 machines? Is it financially advantageous to give them to charity? If we can find them, what is it costing to store them and to insure them? All of these questions, and many more, will go unanswered until such a reconciliation is performed.

Financial managers have the burden of tracking assets, costs, and revenues across time and organizations. For the most part, this is accomplished via the comparison of a plan or schedule to actual results. Unfortunately, the process of tracking and reporting on the value, cost, and utility of distributed IT assets presents challenges that are not encountered when doing the same for a dump truck. IT assets are slippery; they get reassigned, upgraded, retired, folded, spindled, and mutilated. Trying to maintain control of these resources without an asset tracking system is a frustrating and expensive undertaking. Undaunted nonetheless, financial professionals continue their efforts because they understand that maintaining control over the value, acquisition, and disposition of IT assets can substantially improve the financial performance of their organization. Even with this effort, finance professionals frequently don't discover large variances between their fixed-asset accounting system and what is actually in the enterprise until the year-end physical inventory.

With this in mind, consider the value of a monthly analysis showing the IT asset base assigned to the sales department, graphically tracking desktops by processor type across an eight-quarter period. Or consider a simple exception report that provides a monthly departmental breakdown of discovered assets that were not in the previous month's snapshot. Perhaps sorting these new assets by the responsible manager would be useful. To a financial manager struggling to produce an annual inventory, these reports seem impossible, yet they are an effortless by-product of a full-featured asset tracking system.

PURCHASING

Although technically part of the finance department, the purchasing department has a unique perspective—it is responsible for spending the organization's money. And with this charter comes the responsibility of spending it in a manner that optimizes the organization's return on investment.

One of the primary tools the purchasing department uses to carry out its charter is vendor negotiations. For example, a purchasing executive might call in the representative of Clyde's Trucks and say, "Look Clyde, we have 200 of your trucks, and we are projecting a need for fifty-five more. Now what kind of deal will you give me?" On the other hand, the purchasing executive is just as likely to get a call from Clyde announcing that there is a new engine modification available at a very attractive price. In either case, the purchasing executive needs to know the same baseline information. How many Clyde trucks do they own? How many are in service? Are the primary users happy with Clyde's trucks?

Let's switch gears (no pun intended) and consider the same exercise, but now the purchasing executive is dealing with Spreadsheet

Inc. instead of Clyde's Trucks. Spreadsheet Inc.'s records show
that the company owns 11,450 copies of its product. Spreadsheet
Inc. makes a very powerful argument that the installed version of
its product is outdated, harder to use, less powerful, and more difficult to support. Out of the kindness of its heart, Spreadsheet
Inc. offers to discount the upgrade price from $99 down to $49 if
the company agrees to upgrade all copies.

Sounds like a good deal, right? Maybe it is, maybe it's not—but
you can't know unless you are tracking your IT assets. A single
query uncovers that only 3,700 of the 11,450 copies of
Spreadsheet Inc.'s package are installed on the desktops, and even
if you had to pay full price for the 3,700 copies, it would still be
more cost-effective than signing up for 11,450 copies at the attractive $49 price.

After re-focusing negotiations with Spreadsheet Inc. around the
correct number of copies, the purchasing executive turns his attention to a product/vendor analysis. He runs a report showing that
of the 3,700 installed copies of the Spreadsheet Inc. product,
2,100 copies are installed in the marketing department. In
response to this high percentage of use, the purchasing executive
places a telephone call to the IT manager responsible for the marketing department, and informs her of the proposed advantages of
the upgrade. The offer receives a less-than-enthusiastic reception
as the proposed upgrade does not address a major compatibility
problem that marketing is experiencing when using the
Spreadsheet Inc. product with other applications. When
informed of this, the Spreadsheet Inc. representative indicates that
the compatibility issue is addressed in the next revision, and offers
to supply the future release at no additional cost.

With this information in hand, the purchasing executive decides
to make one more check before conducting price negotiations.
He generates a report showing, by department, the number of
installed copies of the product at the beginning of each of the past

six quarters. The analysis shows a steady downward trend across the company in the use of the product. Further, the marketing department shows the steepest decline in use. With this information, the purchasing decision is postponed, and the company conducts an analysis to identify what application and which vendor should replace the Spreadsheet Inc. product.

GENERAL MANAGEMENT

General management's use of an asset tracking system is centered around the organization as a whole. For example, if a company is positioning itself to be acquired or is considering a merger, expansion, downsizing, or expansion through acquisition, then being able to accurately track the number, value, and location of the distributed IT assets would provide significant benefits.

If a company is considering a major expansion, it needs to define the IT infrastructure required to facilitate and support the expansion. To develop an expansion plan, the company must answer several questions: What is the average number of employees per desktop system for each department? What is the average configuration for each department? And, what are the incremental transition costs of the plan?

If a company is planning to downsize, several asset protection and disposal questions must be addressed: What assets will be idle? How can they be redeployed? What surplus assets will we have? What is the value of the surplus assets? Where are the surplus assets located? And, how do we protect them during the downsizing turmoil?

An asset tracking system can also be a valuable tool to facilitate mergers and acquisitions. Companies that frequently entertain acquisitions can require a target company to implement an asset tracking system as part of the due diligence effort. Once installed, the system establishes a benchmark of IT assets at the organization being acquired, preventing assets from "getting lost" during the consolidation, and giving the acquiring IT group a detailed blueprint of the soon-to-be-merged base of technology.

OPERATIONS

For the purposes of this discussion, the overall management of the distributed IT enterprise has been included under the general heading "Operations." This function is usually the responsibility of an IT executive that neither had, nor has, any form of absolute control over the current or future disposition of the distributed enterprise. Yet within these obvious constraints, this brave soul is held accountable for the successful operation of these same resources.

Within the madness of this assignment, a functioning asset tracking system can be a primary link to sanity. For example, a simple request to upgrade all of the marketing department to the latest version of its word processing package comes to the operations executive. Purchasing informs him that the upgrade fee will be $50 per workstation, and that 2,300 workstations need the upgrade. In theory, all that is required is a quick check of the budget to see if marketing has the $115,000 for the upgrade, and the software is ordered.

The French philosopher Voltaire may have had the heart of an IT executive in charge of the distributed enterprise, for he wrote, "Let us work without theorizing, 'tis the only way to make life endurable." Taking Voltaire's lead, the IT executive in the example above will not order the software upgrade until he performs a basic analysis. The questions that need to be answered include: What are the prerequisites for the proposed software upgrade? How many of the workstations do not have the required processor, operating system, memory, or disk space to use the proposed software? What is the cost of upgrading the workstations that do not meet the prerequisites? Without answers to these and other questions, the approval of the upgrade could cascade into a budget crisis, an end-user productivity issue, help desk overload, and a substantial expenditure of IT resources to untangle this string of events. The case study at the conclusion of this chapter graphically illustrates this example.

If the IT executive is to keep even the smallest portion of his or her sanity, then a crystal ball is required. Small insights into the future are critical to keeping the enterprise fully operational. For example, knowing when a file server is within two weeks of exceeding its storage capacity (based on past usage) allows the IT executive to eliminate a production problem before it takes place. Or, when reading in the press that a certain combination of hardware, operating system version, and application can cause problems, the asset tracking system can isolate affected desktops and servers and enable the company to apply a fix before the problem is even encountered.

One of the tools that is part of any attempt to manage the distributed enterprise is electronic software distribution. Electronic software distribution has the ability to make uniform changes across a distributed base of IT assets. There are problems in paradise, however, because—with few exceptions—the enterprise contains desktops with diverse configurations. The challenge then becomes how to prepare distribution packages that address the unique configuration groups within the enterprise. With an asset tracking system, the company can create lists of desktops that meet the prerequisites for a targeted distribution, thereby dramatically reducing the number of failed distributions. Further, by modeling the distribution against the asset tracking repository, variances in configurations can be identified, and packages can be adjusted accordingly.

An asset tracking solution is equally useful to an operations executive who is attempting to maintain a desktop standard. The solution can automatically, or on demand, report any variances from the desired standard configuration or any conditions that may be considered harmful to the desktop.

BUSINESS MANAGEMENT

It may seem like a stretch to include business management as a topic of discussion for an asset tracking system, but consider the following examples before dismissing the possibilities.

A module on the desktop "wakes up" and asks the user to supply information, such as the tag number on the side of the personal computer (PC) or the brand name of the monitor. Taking the concept a step further, the desktop could report the number of records entered in a specific file as a means of determining a data entry clerk's productivity. This information is stored in the asset tracking database along with the user's name, department number, central processing unit (CPU) type, etc., and it is accessed as easily as any other configuration information.

A full-featured asset tracking system can also track non-IT assets that are logically associated with a specific desktop. Desks, chairs, telephones, and fax machines are just a few of the items that can potentially be tracked as part of the distributed enterprise.

A dynamic asset tracking system has the ability to associate any information with a logical desktop. By relating user information (e.g., fax number, mailing address, e-mail address, department, division, employee number, etc.) to the desktop configuration information, the company can establish a virtual link with its personnel via its distributed IT asset repository.

CORPORATE SECURITY

Protecting company assets is often the responsibility of the corporate security department. One of the most difficult tasks corporate security encounters is the protection of the highly liquid, dispersed, and evolving materials that comprise the distributed IT asset base.   The mission of corporate security is not to solve crimes, but to maintain a strong presence that discourages illegal acts. An asset tracking system can flag any server or desktop that fails to make a regular report, as well as those machines that report a missing component. This alert system allows corporate security to be highly visible to all corporate locations by responding to missing assets in a timely manner.

To a security officer, it makes little difference whether the asset was stolen or sent out for repair; the important thing is that those who have access to the asset (employees, contractors, cleaning staff, etc.) are aware that the asset is being tracked and will be promptly discovered when missing. Knowledge that assets are being monitored serves as a strong deterrent to theft.

One of my customers was encouraged to install an asset tracking system after discovering a substantial theft of memory chips and hard disks. The thieves were removing higher-capacity memory chips and disk drives from the desktops and replacing them with lower-capacity components. An active asset tracking system (using Time, Trends, and Null Comparative Anchors) can point corporate security officers to those desktops experiencing reduced configurations. Some of the conditions that can be detected include systems failing to report from one scheduled snapshot to the next, reduced main memory and hard disk storage, and missing communications adapters, video cards, and CD-ROM drives.

CUSTOMER SERVICE/HELP DESK

Most successful IT professionals consider the end-user's time to be their most valued asset. Accordingly, they spend many sleepless hours worrying about how to make the distributed enterprise as productive as possible for the end user. A vice president of a major bank once did the arithmetic for me. He said, "I am responsible for providing desktop technology to 18,000 end users. Fully loaded, each user costs the bank about $105 per hour. Now, if I tie up each of my end users for just one hour per month with non-productive technology issues, it costs the bank $1.89 million." With this idea in mind, most major enterprises have established help desk functions in an effort to quickly remove any IT-related obstacles to end-user productivity. An effective asset tracking system can substantially aid the help desk function by reducing the time it takes to solve end-user problems.

Consider the following example. An end user calls the help desk and gives his first and last name. The help desk professional enters the name into the help desk system, which is linked to an asset tracking repository. Immediately the end-user's name, network address, mailing address, phone number, fax number, and basic system information appear on the screen. The help desk professional asks the end user for the date the problem first appeared and enters it into the asset tracking system.

The asset tracking system immediately displays the deltas between the last known time the end-user's desktop was fully operational and the most recent snapshot of the desktop. The deltas that are displayed include changes in hardware, configuration files, applications installed, and applications deleted. The help desk professional is presented only with the information that has changed, and does not have to wade through a full report on the desktop. By focusing all parties on only those items that were altered, the asset tracking system improves both the productivity of the end user and the help desk professional.

Another advantage offered by an active asset tracking system is that it enables the help desk professional to leverage the knowledge gained through correcting a problem. In the above help desk example, assume the help desk professional determines that the problem is a combination of an older operating system revision (3.1) in conflict with a new application version (6.0). Querying the asset tracking system, the help desk professional can do a quick analysis of all desktops that meet the problem criteria and inform the users of potential problems before they occur. A plan could then be implemented to correct the configuration anomaly.

If the help desk group wants to be more aggressive in preventing problems, it could run an asset tracking analysis to identify those users who are migrating toward the problem (i.e., those running operating system revision 3.1 and application version 5.0). Once found, the help desk would inform users that upgrading their application to 6.0 also requires an operating system upgrade.

LEGAL

An active asset tracking system is a strong indicator to both internal (employees) and external (the Software Publishers Association) sources that you are serious about license compliance. It also delivers the added benefit, should you ever be audited, of providing you with a definitive understanding of all license obligations.

By combining purchasing records and asset tracking information, you can highlight possible license violations before they become an issue. Those conducting such an analysis are often pleasantly surprised to learn that although the company or department is underlicensed on the latest version of a specific package, they are substantially overlicensed on a slightly older revision of the application. In fact, asset tracking systems often find a substantial number of users who have multiple versions of an application installed on the same desktop. Painless compliance is often possible by shifting these slightly older revisions to users who do not require the latest version of an application.

Another legal application of an asset tracking solution concerns the use of the World Wide Web (WWW). There is currently a substantial amount of legal activity centered around employees being exposed to sexually explicit material that is downloaded from the WWW by a manager or co-worker. In chapter 9, we will explore how an effective asset tracking system can detect and prevent such legal liability.

SUMMARY

In better understanding the topic, I built a better mousetrap; in sharing that base of knowledge, I built a better world.

CASE STUDY 2
THE BIG PICTURE

PROLOGUE

ABC Software is a large developer of computer software. It has tight purchasing policies and procedures that are based on a central buying authority. ABC Software primarily relies on acquisitions for its growth, averaging three major acquisitions per year. The general managers of the eleven divisions, and their respective IT professionals, manage the day-to-day operations of division enterprises, including the acquisition of IT resources. A corporate MIS staff, headed by the vice president of information technology, is responsible for the overall design, implementation, and delivery of corporate-wide enterprise services.

ENTERPRISE DEFINITION

ABC Software's distributed enterprise consists of 23,000 desktops, supported by 2,000 servers. The largest concentration of desktops and servers (28 percent) is installed at corporate headquarters. The balance of equipment is located at division headquarters (44 percent) and at various field locations (28 percent).

THE SITUATION/PROBLEM

ABC Software runs its business via the distributed enterprise. Applications include e-mail, order entry, product development, product testing, accounting, revenue forecasts, proposal generation, and hundreds of other applications that rely on the enterprise to share and consolidate information. With this dependence comes the challenge of keeping the various divisions, departments, and geographic locations synchronized as they experience varying rates of growth and as they adopt diverse technologies.

If ABC Software is to continue its rapid pace of expansion and its dependence on the distributed enterprise, a means must be found to bring an enterprise vision to the various senior managers within the divisions. These autonomous managers must be convinced that by considering the enterprise beyond their own boundaries, they too can be better served. To succeed, ABC Software must establish the enterprise as an entity that transcends individual departments or divisions.

THREE-STEP PROCESS

Before introducing the senior management team to the problems and dynamics of the corporate enterprise, care must be taken first to level set their knowledge of their own organizations. This requires, for some period of time, that managers be given a concise and consistent analysis of the IT resources in their divisional enterprises. The format of this analysis should be constant across all divisions.

Once this analysis has been distributed on a regular basis (e.g., semimonthly over a one-year period), managers are encouraged to look for trends within their divisions.

The final step is to compare and contrast trends of various divisional enterprises to each other and against the business plans of those business units and the corporation as a whole.

THE ANALYSIS

It is critical that the analysis be easily "digested" and presented on a single page so the results can be compared over time. For instance, managers can lay out six of these one-page, easy-to-interpret analyses end to end to obtain an immediate view of asset trends during the past six months across their organization. Multiple-page reports or tedious reporting methods inhibit this type of trend analysis.

A nearly ideal analysis that compares a specified division to the entire corporation is described on the following pages. There are five sections to this report, each providing its own insight into the subenterprise. *Note: Although such a report would ideally appear on a single page, for formatting purposes, this book presents the sections in a series.*

IT ASSET ALLOCATION ANALYSIS: LAN PRODUCTS DIVISION

IT ASSET ALLOCATION ANALYSIS — SUMMARY

The first section provides a framework for understanding the remaining sections.

SUMMARY

There are 4,118 workstations in the LAN Products Division supported by 275 servers. The workstations have a total of 2,471 GB of hard disk storage, of which 82 percent is used, leaving 18 percent available for future use. The servers have a total of 1,100 GB of hard disk storage, of which 73 percent is used, leaving 27 percent available for future use.

The average workstation has 600 MB of hard disk storage and is at 82 percent of capacity. The average server has 4,000 MB of hard disk storage and is at 73 percent of capacity.

There is, on average, a minus 4 MB difference in installed RAM and a minus 95 MB difference in hard disk storage between the LAN Products Division and the remainder of the corporation.

IT ASSET ALLOCATION ANALYSIS — OPERATING SYSTEM DISTRIBUTION

The second section of the analysis presents the division management with the broadest measurement of desktop utility—the operating system.

The following graph establishes the distribution of operating systems within the division and, as a point of reference (Reflective Comparative Anchor), contrasts this distribution against the balance of the corporation.

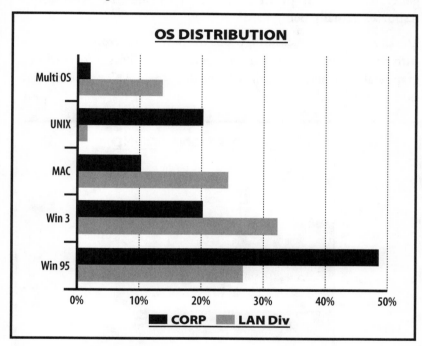

In examining this second section, the business unit executive may, for the first time, gain a broad understanding of the division's technology base and how it blends with the rest of the corporate enterprise. Questions that are raised after just a brief review of the above chart include: Why are so many of the LAN products division's workstations carrying the overhead of multiple operating systems? Are there benefits to using UNIX that the LAN products division is not aware of? What makes us so dependent on the Macintosh platform? And, why is the LAN products division's migration from Windows 3 to Windows 95 so far behind the rest of the corporation?

IT Asset Allocation Analysis — Top Applications Distribution

The third section of the analysis answers the obvious question generated by the previous chart—how are the workstation resources actually being used?

Usually once the technology platform is understood, questions turn to how the workstations are being used. This information is graphically displayed, again contrasting the LAN products division with the balance of the corporation.

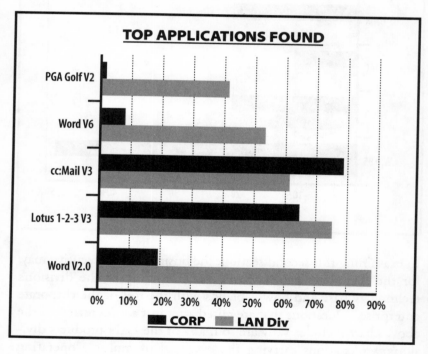

Once you know what applications populate the desktops, you can understand the utility of the desktops and you can understand the application compatibility between users. This will help you more effectively plan hardware and software upgrades. Questions that might follow a brief review of the previous chart include: What does PGA Golf have to do with the mission of this division? Why are we running two versions of Word? And, what is the corporation using for word processing? Considering that a large number of desktops have two word processors and PGA Golf installed, is the proposed disk upgrade really necessary?

IT ASSET ALLOCATION ANALYSIS — CPU DISTRIBUTION

The fourth section of the analysis anchors the operating system and application sections to the base of hardware technology.

By examining the previous two sections of the analysis in light of the installed base of hardware technology, we can begin to establish a "cause and effect relationship" between the various components of the desktop enterprise.

As we saw earlier, the LAN products division is substantially behind the rest of the corporation in upgrading to new operating system versions. It also appears that the LAN products division is out of step in its selection of a word processing standard. These anomalies could be the result of business practices, or they could be tied to the limitations of the hardware platforms. If, for example, Windows 95 and/or Word 6.0 required a faster processor than was installed across the division, a natural consequence of having the slower base of processors would be to run older versions of less resource-intensive software.

The following chart highlights the fact that the LAN products division is behind in adopting new hardware technology as well.

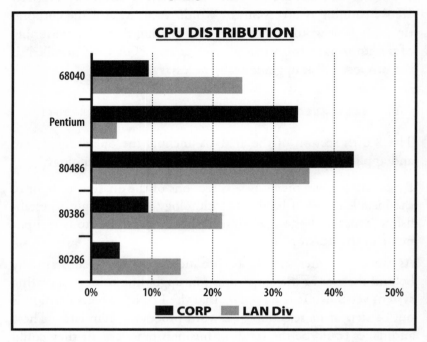

The fundamental question: Is the LAN products division running older technology because its application base does not require additional processor capacity, or is it missing out on the end-user productivity gained through installing the latest software revisions because of hardware restrictions?

Before studying the impact of processor capacity on business productivity, a broad understanding of other "technology gateways" is required. Often the capacity of the desktop is limited by factors not related to processor speed. The final two sections of this analysis highlight these factors.

IT ASSET ALLOCATION ANALYSIS — RAM CAPACITY

The fifth section of this analysis highlights how much random access memory (RAM) is installed on the LAN products division's desktops, and contrasts it with the corporation desktops. This is especially important as many applications, and/or combinations of applications, require a certain amount of RAM.

The above graph continues to highlight the fact that the LAN products division has substantially fewer capable desktops when compared to the rest of the corporation. This may be the result of not needing additional memory to run the desired complement of applications, the fact that the installed CPU base does not support additional RAM, or budget considerations. Regardless of the reason, knowing the RAM complement can be invaluable as additional applications, corporate or division inspired, are considered.

IT ASSET ALLOCATION ANALYSIS — HARD DISK CAPACITY

The last section of this analysis highlights the status of hard disk storage for the LAN products division's desktops.

Hard disk storage is important because all desktop applications that are resident on the desktop consume disk space and require some form of "working margin" to complete their tasks. In addition, considering the declining prices of online storage, it is rarely cost-efficient to burden end users with the task of juggling limited storage capacity.

The above graph follows the earlier trends in that the LAN products division is again underconfigured when compared to the rest of the corporate enterprise. Of greater interest than the average hard disk capacity is the delta in free space available between the LAN products division and the corporation. Should the corporation want to distribute an application or data file to the enterprise that requires ninety megabytes of hard disk space, the LAN products division would find its technology base awkwardly out of step with the rest of the enterprise.

BUILDING ENTERPRISE KNOWLEDGE

Providing the senior management team of ABC's LAN products division with the above analysis has given team members new insight into the composition, application, and risks associated with their enterprise configuration. As mentioned earlier, all of the sections of this analysis would ideally appear on a single page. With such a consolidation (see the figure below), over time, the management of the LAN products division can gain insight into their enterprise and how it relates to the corporate enterprise. By regularly running this analysis and posting the results side by side on a wall, trends can easily be identified.

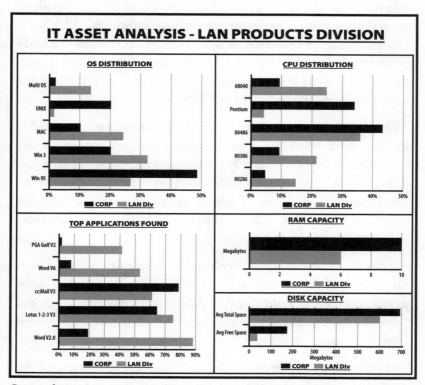

Once the senior management team is accustomed to thinking of its IT asset base as an entity, cross-division sharing of the above analysis can be instituted. This draws all parties closer to recognizing the value of coordinating their efforts, and introduces the corporate enterprise into the divisional IT decision process.

An epilogue is included in this hypothetical case study to highlight some of the discoveries that MIS professionals have shared with me in the management of their distributed enterprise.

As a result of reviewing the IT Asset Allocation Analysis, the LAN products division's management learns that:

• The LAN products division, which was created as the result of several acquisitions, has multiple desktop standards. This partly explains the distribution of operating systems across the LAN products division enterprise. Management forms a task group to investigate the cost and business advantages of standardizing on a single operating system environment.

• The corporation recently negotiated a favorable contract with a leading word processor provider whose product requires fewer resources, has an easier user interface, and offers greater compatibility across platforms than the word processor installed in the LAN products division. As a result, management establishes standards within the LAN products division based on the favorable word processor.

• An investigation prompted by the analysis reveals that more than 80 percent of the employee base has PGA Golf, as well as other games, on their desktops. LAN products division management takes the appropriate action to ensure that all games are removed from employees' desktops.

• The technology gap between the LAN products division and the corporation highlights the fact that the division is falling dangerously behind the technology curve, impacting employee productivity. Therefore, management adjusts the budget to channel more resources into a planned upgrade of the LAN products division enterprise.

FROM THEORY TO APPLICATION

This case study describes a seemingly utopian situation of the division heads lining up behind the natural needs of the corporate enterprise. Before dismissing this possibility, consider the fact that it is in the "selfish" interests of each division to make the "corporate" decisions regarding their individual enterprises. It is by bringing together "pictures" of the individual interests, in a common format to form a picture of the whole, that everyone can share a vision.

Consider how the above concept might fit into the annual corporate planning process. Most major corporations gather their department and division managers together once each year to document the coming year's corporate objectives and to discuss the strategic and operational options that are critical to reaching those targets. If the IT Asset Allocation Analysis is run once a month for each division (as in Case Study 2), and corporate objectives are defined, then linking the two to make the corporate enterprise a point of discussion during the planning process would simply be a matter of presentation.

One means of presenting this information during the planning process is to commandeer a wall. At the top of the wall, in banner form, is a list of the summarized corporate objectives. Beneath this banner of objectives are the six bimonthly reports sorted by date and division. The effectiveness of this presentation is best conveyed via the illustration on the following page:

CORPORATE OBJECTIVES

Revenue Growth, Profits, Cost Containment, Acquisitions,
ROI, ROA, Downsizing, Reorganization, Expansion, etc.

(DIVISION TRENDS)

DIVISION 1 IT ASSET ANALYSIS	DIVISION 2 IT ASSET ANALYSIS	DIVISION 3 IT ASSET ANALYSIS	DIVISION 4 IT ASSET ANALYSIS	DIVISION 5 IT ASSET ANALYSIS	SEPT. (NOW)
DIVISION 1 IT ASSET ANALYSIS	DIVISION 2 IT ASSET ANALYSIS	DIVISION 3 IT ASSET ANALYSIS	DIVISION 4 IT ASSET ANALYSIS	DIVISION 5 IT ASSET ANALYSIS	JULY
DIVISION 1 IT ASSET ANALYSIS	DIVISION 2 IT ASSET ANALYSIS	DIVISION 3 IT ASSET ANALYSIS	DIVISION 4 IT ASSET ANALYSIS	DIVISION 5 IT ASSET ANALYSIS	MAY
DIVISION 1 IT ASSET ANALYSIS	DIVISION 2 IT ASSET ANALYSIS	DIVISION 3 IT ASSET ANALYSIS	DIVISION 4 IT ASSET ANALYSIS	DIVISION 5 IT ASSET ANALYSIS	MARCH
DIVISION 1 IT ASSET ANALYSIS	DIVISION 2 IT ASSET ANALYSIS	DIVISION 3 IT ASSET ANALYSIS	DIVISION 4 IT ASSET ANALYSIS	DIVISION 5 IT ASSET ANALYSIS	JAN.
DIVISION 1 IT ASSET ANALYSIS	DIVISION 2 IT ASSET ANALYSIS	DIVISION 3 IT ASSET ANALYSIS	DIVISION 4 IT ASSET ANALYSIS	DIVISION 5 IT ASSET ANALYSIS	NOV. (LAST YEAR)

(TIME-BASED ENTERPRISE VIEW)

Using this format, the division enterprises and the enterprise as a whole can be examined in light of the corporate mission. The vertical rows show the technology trend of a specific division, allowing you to determine if the current trend within a division is in harmony with the corporate objectives. The horizontal rows give you a picture of the corporate enterprise at a given moment in time, providing answers to questions such as, What did the enterprise look like when we did the reorganization last January?

A discussion of the IT Asset Allocation Analysis contained in Case Study 2, whether part of an annual plan or some other forum, is invaluable in focusing the distributed enterprise management team on the larger issues facing the corporate information technology base. This is by no means the only way to coordinate such an effort, but it is an easy and time-efficient medium that allows for a quantitative discussion of the issues.

CHAPTER 5

• POODLES AND DOBERMANS •

Me: I'm looking to buy a dog.

Dog Breeder: What kind of dog are you looking for?

Me: I'm looking for a smart, active, low-maintenance, easy-to-train, aggressive watchdog that is good with kids.

Dog Breeder: So am I, and if I find one, I plan to marry him.

As in my quest for a dog, perfection often involves contradiction. As the breeder would explain to me, "Smart dogs are often more difficult to train as they are distracted by all of the possibilities that surround them, aggressive dogs and children do not belong in the same sentence, and low-maintenance and active go together like oil and water." And so, in my quest for a dog some twenty-five years ago, I failed to describe a plausible dog, but achieved near perfection in describing the ideal functional qualities of an asset tracking system.

For those of you not fixated on dogs, let me translate these qualities into something you can identify with. An effective asset tracking system must be able to automatically translate its data into insightful analyses (smart). It must be able to accumulate and use multiple data points for each item it tracks (active). It should be a silent servant, not imposing any administrative burden on its owner (low maintenance). As it is impossible to anticipate all of the ways an asset tracking system can be used, it must provide easily accessible, ad hoc reporting (easy to train). It should actively audit the enterprise, searching for conditions that you deem to be harmful or questionable (aggressive watchdog). And most important, it must be transparent to the end users and server administrators (good with kids).

I have taken the time to define each of the above points in greater detail. Some of the topics will become more lucid as you review the case studies. But before flipping to the case studies, I encourage you to read this chapter as it gives you a look at the whole dog—I promise this is the last dog analogy—and the possibilities that exist in a properly designed system.

ANALYSIS (SMART)

Analysis is the art of seeing the steps to a conclusion and logically presenting the information required in a format that facilitates a decision. Analysis does not focus on the specific, but rather defines the field of play. Regardless of the size of your enterprise or the nature of your business, there are specific analyses that apply to common functions within each organization. For example, the operations department needs to know the true cost and end-user impact of upgrading an application. Finance needs analyses comparing the asset base over different time periods. Purchasing needs vendor trend analyses. And legal demands license compliance analyses. Each of these analyses requires progressive steps of gathering data, and through organized methods, turning that data into information.

For example, if you want to compute the cost of upgrading the finance department to the latest version of a spreadsheet, you would ultimately need to go through the following process:

1) Ascertain the number of desktops in finance.

2) Determine how many desktops use the spreadsheet.

3) Determine if any of them already have the proposed upgrade.

4) Determine the prerequisites (CPU speed, memory, free disk space, operating system revision) for the new revision of the spreadsheet.

5) Apply the prerequisites against the end users who require the new spreadsheet version in order to determine which users need system upgrades as part of their spreadsheet upgrade.

6) Once the required quantity of upgrade components (CPU speed, memory, free disk space, operating system revision) is known, research the cost for each of the upgrade components, including the spreadsheet upgrade. Note: Knowing the quantities of the components required allows you to spend the majority of your time scrubbing the costs of components that have the greatest impact on the total cost of the upgrade.

7) Isolate (compute by cost type) the various cost components to determine if further research is warranted and to ascertain the operational feasibility of the upgrade.

8) Ascertain the impact of such an upgrade on user productivity (downtime in implementing the upgrade), as well as the IT resources required to implement the proposed change.

9) Solicit the additional specific information required to facilitate the upgrade or justify canceling the program.

The above nine steps show how an analysis is executed, one step at a time. If your asset tracking system had a comprehensive set of analyses, you could accomplish all of the above in a two-step process:

1) Identify the department, its package prerequisites, and their estimated costs.

2) Print or display the analysis.

Ideally, this system-generated analysis should present its findings in a manner that follows the human thought process. It should make optimum use of text, tables, and graphs to facilitate a decision. For an example of a system-generated analysis, see the case study at the end of this chapter.

SAMPLING OF DATA POINTS (ACTIVE)

An asset inventory tells you what your distributed enterprise looks like at a given moment in time. An asset tracking system tells you the current state of the enterprise, where it has been, and the direction in which it is evolving. This is accomplished through the capture and maintenance of multiple snapshots of the asset base over time, allowing for both a regression and sensitivity analysis of the distributed enterprise. These analyses can be focused at the desktop level, enterprise level, or any level in between.

Without this time-based gathering of asset information, much of what has been discussed in earlier chapters (Time Comparative Anchors, Trends Comparative Anchors, Null Comparative Anchors, corporate security examples, purchasing examples, etc.), would not be possible. Having an active asset tracking system that accumulates snapshots of individual items over time allows you to gain insight in three ways:

• It allows you to view all or part of your network at a given moment in time and compare it to some event external to the asset tracking system. What type of desktop (processor type) was the branch banking software originally deployed on? How many new servers did we install in Europe last year? Who was the last person to install XYZ application? These are examples of questions that link time and an external event or structure.

• It allows you to compare multiple snapshots of the same item and develop a trend or comparison. What is the growth rate of word processor X? What is the growth rate in end-user hard disk storage over the past six quarters? Which desktops are reporting a decline in main memory since the last snapshot? These are the types of questions that draw on historical trends within individual items.

- It allows you to draw comparisons between different items during the same or different time periods, creating new insights. How has the distribution of word processor applications across job classifications changed over the past two years? Over the past three years, what is the frequency of main memory upgrades for users who today have three or more Microsoft products? The possibilities for combining data items into meaningful insights is infinite.

Once the power of having historical snapshots of individual items is understood, the question arises as to how often snapshots (inventories of the desktops and servers associated with a specific date) should be taken. This decision will be influenced by several factors:

- How difficult is it to take a snapshot of the enterprise? Asset tracking systems that place a heavy administrative burden on the IT resources are labor intensive. Asset tracking systems that require end-user involvement will, out of necessity, restrict the frequency of snapshots.

- How heavy is the network load? Asset tracking systems that use the network to gather snapshots will necessarily put an additional burden on the network. This traffic can be minimized by batching these snapshots at the server level and then sending them to a central repository. Using non-peak hours can also minimize network strains. If using non-peak hours is a consideration, you should avoid using asset tracking systems that send snapshots as part of a startup sequence because most networks are under heavy use during startup hours.

- For many organizations, the ideal snapshot frequency is implemented around a "revolving schedule." A revolving schedule takes snapshots of some percentage of the enterprise on a regular schedule, completing a full-enterprise inventory over a desirable interval. For example, if a company optimally wanted weekly snapshots of the enterprise, but because of network constraints a full-enterprise inventory was only feasible once a month, a revolving schedule may be the answer. Using a revolving schedule, snapshots would be taken of one-seventh of the enterprise each night. This would distribute network load and allow for a weekly update of the enterprise. A perceived drawback of this methodology is that the enterprise is not captured in unison at a given moment in time. This is true, but in most cases the value of having more frequent updates far outweighs the lack of perfect synchronization.

The value of end-user time is a major consideration in determining the frequency of snapshots. With few exceptions, the greater the concern for end-user productivity, the more frequent the snapshots. This observation is tied to improving help desk response, to reacting quickly to upgrades and enhancements to the enterprise, and to being responsive to the business needs of the functional organizations.

Often, a critical reporting requirement will dictate the snapshot schedule. For example, an insurance company may need to verify the state of all desktops that are involved in policy writing once each week.

ADMINISTRATION
(LOW MAINTENANCE)

An asset tracking system should not create additional burdens in managing the enterprise. Specifically, it should be easy to install at all levels. This includes the central repository, servers, and desktops. This one-time installation may seem like a small consideration, but depending on the architecture of the system selected, the implementation costs can be ten times the cost of the asset tracking system!

One of the best ways to avoid surprises in this area is to purchase a two-server, 100-client version of the proposed system and install it prior to committing to a full-enterprise implementation. This is cheap insurance, as the experience gained in this limited installation may lead you to reconsider the system you selected and/or the means of deployment. For more information on implementation issues, see chapter 10.

Ideally, administration of the enterprise asset repository should be a "lights-out" operation. No human intervention should be required when a new desktop is reported to the repository or when a new item (element) is discovered on a desktop or server. With the exception of telling the system you want it to begin tracking a new element of information, the system should gather its information on a predetermined schedule, totally unattended.

EASILY ACCESSIBLE, AD HOC REPORTING (EASY TO TRAIN)

As mentioned earlier, it is impossible to predict all of the uses for an enterprise-wide IT asset tracking system. Within this uncertainty, however, there is vast opportunity. As psychologist Erich Fromm said in *Man For Himself*, "The quest for certainty blocks the search for meaning. Uncertainty is the very condition to impel man to unfold his powers." If the full power of an enterprise asset tracking system is to be "unfolded," the raw information in the repository must be accessible at three levels:

TO THE IT TECHNICAL PROFESSIONAL

This professional, through writing code or using specialized data extraction tools (e.g., structured query language [SQL] tools), should have infinite flexibility in manipulating the repository. This ability is key as each organization and enterprise is unique, and there is no system or solution that can anticipate all of the value to be derived from the captured information.

With this flexibility, consideration must be given to the human resources that manage the enterprise. To effectively leverage the IT technical professional, the information within the repository should be well documented and easily accessible.

To Non-technical Management

The system should provide an interface to tool sets that enable managers to easily extract information that is relevant to their responsibilities. In chapter 4, we saw how the purchasing, finance, corporate security, help desk, operations, general management, and legal departments could make valuable use of an asset tracking repository. Some of the information these department managers need may only be met with the assistance of an IT technical professional; however, with an easy user interface, these managers can directly access the repository and gain insights that allow them to quickly make informed decisions.

User tools in this area include easy-to-use report writers, canned reports that allow users to change predefined variables, and the ability to export information directly into a "user-enabled environment" such as a spreadsheet.

To Other Applications

An effective implementation of an asset tracking solution allows other systems management tools and applications to extend their functionality. Assuming the proper architecture, the asset repository can easily export information or provide a "live link" to other operations. This topic is covered in greater detail in chapter 6.

ACTIVELY AUDIT THE ENTERPRISE
(AGGRESSIVE WATCHDOG)

Every good asset tracking system should come with its own auditor. Once the asset tracking system is installed, the auditor—green eyeshade, armbands and all—should somehow be digitized and injected into the enterprise. This auditor should do what all auditors do: use his or her training and experience to monitor and report dangerous, or potentially dangerous, situations. Without the technology to digitize a human auditor, the next best option is to use our knowledge of what is dangerous, or potentially dangerous, to the enterprise, along with the "legs" of an asset tracking system, to create an electronic auditor. The auditing function should be viewed as a major and necessary component of any asset tracking system.

This electronic auditing function should allow you to easily define conditions you want audited and then, either automatically or upon request, conduct an audit that reports on those desktops and servers that fail to meet the audit criteria. There is an unlimited number of uses for the audit function, but most fall into one of four categories:

ENFORCEMENT OF STANDARDS

The most obvious use of the auditor is the enforcement of desktop standards. The advantage to having an asset tracking system do the audit is that it can tell you not only when a system falls out of standards, but it can also tell you specifically how it fails to meet desired criteria.

TARGETED BUSINESS REQUIREMENTS

You may wish to be informed whenever a file server exceeds 85 percent capacity. A business unit manager may have a productivity problem and wish to be informed when users have games installed on their systems. Any targeted item, or combination of items, can become part of an audit.

PREVENTIVE MEASURES

As you discover problems within the enterprise (via the help desk, business managers, or suppliers), you can have the auditor monitor the enterprise and report new occurrences of the condition. This allows those operating the enterprise to be proactive and disarm problems before they manifest.

EDUCATE THE USER BASE

Another powerful use of an auditor is education. For example, it was discovered that the latest version (Version 3.25) of an operating system is incompatible with Spreadsheet Inc.'s Version 6. With an auditor, every current and future user of Version 6 spreadsheet could be warned not to upgrade their operating system to Version 3.25. We read about dozens of alerts from software vendors each week; the auditor gives you the ability to apply this knowledge to the enterprise.

TRANSPARENT TO THE END USER AND SERVER ADMINISTRATOR (GOOD WITH KIDS)

With a single exception, the asset tracking system should be transparent to end users and server administrators. The exception should be a facility allowing the end user or administrator to take a snapshot on demand. This on-demand snapshot allows the end user or server administrator to send the help desk professional an up-to-the-minute snapshot of the problem desktop or server.

SUMMARY

An effective "system" is nothing more than a feedback loop, providing effortless answers and insights into the questions it generates.

CASE STUDY 3
THE DRIBBLE EFFECT

PROLOGUE

Mega Bank is a large bank that has an active acquisition strategy. It averages one large merger/acquisition each year and one small acquisition each quarter. Mega Bank's business model calls for a distributed enterprise that is managed via a corporate MIS function. There is a hierarchical MIS structure that has dotted-line reporting to the various business unit executives. The design and management of the distributed enterprise falls under the senior vice president of information resources, with funding sign-off required by the individual business units. Major modifications to the structure of the enterprise and/or substantial changes to the quality of delivered services are managed at the senior vice president level via the quarterly and annual planning processes.

ENTERPRISE DEFINITION

Mega Bank's distributed enterprise consists of 60,000 desktops, supported by 3,600 servers. The largest concentration of desktops and servers (46 percent) is installed in the greater New York City area. The three major division headquarters locations represent 24 percent of the distributed enterprise, branch operations 20 percent, and international operations 10 percent.

Due to its merger/acquisition strategy over the past three years, Mega Bank has experienced a 27 percent compound annual growth rate in the number of servers and desktops supported as part of the distributed enterprise. In addition, although migrating toward a standard server and workstation paradigm, Mega Bank has been required to expand its enterprise definition to support two new server platforms and three new desktop platforms.

THE SITUATION/PROBLEM

Mega Bank's successful expansion program has had the undesirable effect of increasing the unplanned annual desktop and server expenditures from $90 per desktop to $207 per desktop. The majority of this 230 percent increase (from $5.4 million to $12.4 million) in unbudgeted expenses falls into five upgrade categories: software, memory, CPU (processor), hard disk (online storage), and operating system.

A cursory review has determined that the primary source of unplanned spending is the upgrading of application software to a new revision. These upgrades often have prerequisites that exceed the recommended individual desktop configurations and require the user to request additional memory, hard disk storage, operating system software, or processing capacity in order to effectively run the new version of the application software.

ACTION PLAN

Having recently installed a comprehensive asset tracking system, the senior vice president of information resources directs that all future software upgrades involving more than 100 desktops have a "full-cost model" of the upgrade prepared prior to the upgrade decision. On the third of October, the first proposed upgrade to fall under this policy is received from the finance department. The purchase order requisition calls for upgrading 2,229 copies of Spreadsheet Inc.'s spreadsheet application to Version 6.0 for $111,450 ($50 per copy). The analysis, which ultimately does not support this request, is detailed below.

THE ANALYSIS

As in the previous case studies, it is important that the provided analysis be easily "digested" and presented on a single page. In this Software Upgrade Analysis, having the information on a single page affords the reader two advantages. First, it allows the reader to view the relationship between the various elements of the report. And second, it allows the reader to quickly scan a large number of upgrade requests and focus attention only on those that have the greatest impact.

A nearly ideal Software Upgrade Analysis is diagrammed on the following pages. There are five sections to this report, each providing its own insight into the proposed upgrade. *Note: Although such a report would ideally appear on a single page, for formatting purposes, this book presents the sections in a series.*

Before beginning the Software Upgrade Analysis, the asset tracking system needs some information about the proposed upgrade. This information is summarized in the fourth section of the analysis (see the illustration on the following page entitled Change Analysis), but is included here, out of order, as a means of summarizing the input prompted by the asset tracking system as part of the analysis preparation.

CHANGE ANALYSIS

DEPARTMENT - **FINANCE**
APPLICATION - **SPREADSHEET 6.0**
DESCRIPTION : ANALYSIS OF THE RESOURCES REQUIRED TO
UPGRADE THE FINANCE DEPARTMENT TO SPREADSHEET 6.0.

PREREQUISITES

MEMORY - **8192K**
CPU - **486**
FREE DISK - **16MB**
SOFTWARE - **SPREADSHEET 1.0**
O.S. - **WIN 3.11**

COST DATA

UPGRADE TO SPREADSHEET 6.0 - **$50**
OPERATING SYSTEM UPGRADE - **$75**
MEMORY UPGRADE - **$200**
MEMORY UPGRADE UNIT - **8MB**
DISK UPGRADE - **$200**
DISK UPGRADE UNIT - **600MB**
CPU UPGRADE - **$1,200**
LABOR - **$95/HR**
LOST PRODUCTIVITY - **$105/HR**

TIME REQUIRED (HOURS)

SPREADSHEET 6.0 - **3**
OPERATING SYSTEM UPGRADE - **5**
MEMORY UPGRADE - **2**
DISK UPGRADE - **4**
CPU UPGRADE - **6**

The information highlighted in bold type was entered by the person running the analysis. Ideally, the person running the analysis should be able to either directly enter the prompted value or select the value from a list provided by the asset tracking system. Once this information has been entered, the analysis is generated.

SOFTWARE UPGRADE ANALYSIS

SOFTWARE UPGRADE ANALYSIS — SUMMARY

The first section of this analysis, the Summary, provides an overview of the proposed upgrade.

SUMMARY

There are 2,229 desktops (workstations and servers) in the Finance Department. Of these, 29 already have Version 6.0 installed, and 80 do not meet the specified eligibility requirements. No costs are calculated for these desktops. Of the remaining 2,120 eligible desktops, 1,420 meet the specified prerequisites, and only require the new software version at a cost of $71,000. Additionally, upgrading these 1,420 desktops will result in a direct labor cost of $404,700 and a lost productivity cost of $447,300. The other 700 eligible desktops fail to meet at least one prerequisite and require an operating system and/or hardware upgrade in addition to the new software version, at a cost of $680,025. Additionally, upgrading these 700 desktops will result in a direct labor cost of $689,225 and a lost productivity cost of $761,775. The total cost of implementing this upgrade is $3,054,025.

The person responsible for analyzing the request to upgrade the spreadsheet application in the finance department need only look at the purchase requisition for $111,450 and the last number in the Summary, $3,054,025, to determine the need for further consideration. In this case, the Summary indicates that the actual cost of upgrading finance to be more than twenty-seven times higher than the requested amount.

Having determined a wide variance between the proposed cost and the estimated cost, an examination of the other sections of the analysis is warranted.

SOFTWARE UPGRADE ANALYSIS — DESKTOP DISTRIBUTION

The second section of the analysis (see illustration entitled Desktop Distribution) provides a high-level breakdown of the upgrade across the desktops. This is especially useful to those who are responsible for installing and supporting the upgraded systems. Desktops that demand a hardware and/or operating system modification as part of an application upgrade usually require a disproportionate amount of support resources. This knowledge can be invaluable in planning for the implementation and help desk resources required to support the proposed application upgrade. The following chart quickly tells those responsible for supporting the enterprise that a significant portion, 700, of the users upgrading this application will require substantial technical support services.

Support resources and the cost of materials only tell part of the story for these 700 desktops that need to be modified before receiving the Spreadsheet 6.0 upgrade. The associated impact on user productivity, as illustrated in Section 3, Cost Breakdown, may be the most significant factor in determining the feasibility and methodology of an application upgrade.

SOFTWARE UPGRADE ANALYSIS — COST BREAKDOWN

Section 1 and Section 2 provide a high-level understanding of the cost and support requirements for the proposed upgrade. Section 3 presents a cross section of detail summarizing the proposed upgrade, both by expense components and type of expense. It is in this section that the impact of labor expenses and the cost of lost productivity are introduced. These numbers are calculated from the entered values as summarized in Section 4, Change Analysis.

Before examining the results in Section 3, there are two columns of information, "Labor" and "Lost Productivity," that deserve special consideration because they represent items that are often overlooked when calculating the cost of an application upgrade. The "Labor" column includes the salary expense (i.e., the fully loaded labor rate) of the IT professionals supporting the effort. The "Lost Productivity" column includes the labor expense for the end user, plus some lost opportunity tied to how much product or revenue the employee will be unable to produce as a result of not having access to the desktop. For example, a telesales person who is separated from the desktop for two hours may have a fully loaded cost to the company of $200, but during that same two hours have the ability to generate $1,000 of revenue/orders. In this example, I have kept the hourly rate at an extremely conservative $105 in order to show that even a low number can have a profound impact.

As the following chart illustrates, "Labor" and "Lost Productivity" substantially exceed the cost of purchasing the required hardware and software. The two columns represent nearly half of the projected cost of the undertaking. Further, the total in the "Materials" column highlights the cost of implementing the 700 users who do not meet the hardware and software prerequisites of the proposed spreadsheet upgrade. Here we discover the reason that the $680,025 material cost of the upgrade is more than six times the original budget estimate of $111,450.

COST BREAKDOWN FOR THE 700 DESKTOPS FAILING PREREQUISITES					
ITEM	UNIT	MATERIALS	LABOR	LOST PRODUCTIVITY	TOTAL
MEMORY	580	$116,000	$110,200	$121,800	$348,000
CPU	396	$475,200	$225,720	$249,480	$950,400
SOFTWARE	700	$35,000	$199,500	$220,500	$455,000
HARD DISKS	211	$42,200	$80,180	$88,620	$211,000
OS	155	$11,625	$73,625	$81,375	$166,625
TOTAL	N/A	$680,025	$689,225	$761,775	$2,131,025

After reviewing the results of the Cost Breakdown, most individuals are shocked at the projected cost of the upgrade. It is for this reason that an effective analysis provides the manager with a review of the values that were the basis of the analysis. Here, if errors were made, they can be corrected and the analysis rerun to reflect those corrections.

Software Upgrade Analysis — Change Analysis
(Duplicate)

CHANGE ANALYSIS

DEPARTMENT - **FINANCE**
APPLICATION - **SPREADSHEET 6.0**
DESCRIPTION : ANALYSIS OF THE RESOURCES REQUIRED TO
UPGRADE THE FINANCE DEPARTMENT TO SPREADSHEET 6.0.

PREREQUISITES

MEMORY - **8192K**
CPU - **486**
FREE DISK - **16MB**
SOFTWARE - **SPREADSHEET 1.0**
O.S. - **WIN 3.11**

COST DATA

UPGRADE TO SPREADSHEET 6.0 - **$50**
OPERATING SYSTEM UPGRADE - **$75**
MEMORY UPGRADE - **$200**
MEMORY UPGRADE UNIT - **8MB**
DISK UPGRADE - **$200**
DISK UPGRADE UNIT - **600MB**
CPU UPGRADE - **$1,200**
LABOR - **$95/HR**
LOST PRODUCTIVITY - **$105/HR**

TIME REQUIRED (HOURS)

SPREADSHEET 6.0 - **3**
OPERATING SYSTEM UPGRADE - **5**
MEMORY UPGRADE - **2**
DISK UPGRADE - **4**
CPU UPGRADE - **6**

In revisiting Section 4, we can now focus on those areas that have the greatest cost impact to the project. In this case, special attention would be given to the CPU and memory costs because they represent the largest unplanned expense items.

Section 5 highlights the expense distribution (excluding labor and lost productivity costs) of the upgrade. The pie chart graphically compares each cost component to the total projected expense.

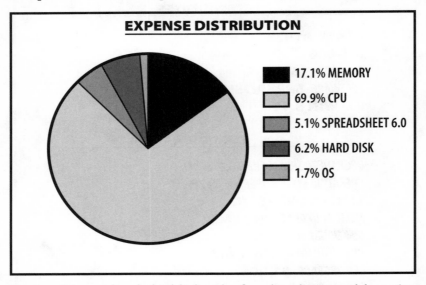

Section 5 immediately highlights the fact that the Spreadsheet 6.0 application portion of the proposed upgrade is only 5.1 percent of the total cost of upgrading the spreadsheet software on finance's desktops. In fact, from a cost perspective, based on the variables provided and documented in Section 4, this upgrade has more to do with upgrading the central processing units than all other factors.

It is when examining these relationships that Sections 4 and 5 work together. Having an automated analysis allows those entering the variables to minimize the time they spend researching the cost of the various upgrade components. In this example, the person entered an operating system upgrade cost of $75 and a CPU-upgrade cost of $1,200. These were rough estimates and fall within a rational sampling of market prices.

Both of these cost items, however, are highly configuration dependent. The true cost of upgrading either the operating system or the CPU hinges on the specific workstation starting and ending point. Clearly, an in-depth analysis of each cost component and the computation of a precise average cost for each item is possible. The luxury of having an asset tracking system should, however, save you extensive research on the cost of each component.

Consider the following questions that can be answered with just the rough approximations that were entered. With an estimated materials and labor expense of more than $1.8 million and a total cost, including lost productivity, of more than $3 million, does it make sense to give this upgrade further consideration? Based on the cost distribution, does it make sense to spend time fine-tuning any of the cost values other than the cost of upgrading the application and processor? Considering the cost of this upgrade, is there a more cost-effective way to meet the users' needs that does not involve Spreadsheet 6.0? What if you found a way to cut the cost of CPU upgrades by 40 percent? Would any of the answers to the above questions change?

By comparing and contrasting the information contained in Sections 4 and 5, iterative analyses can be run, establishing "sensitivity parameters" that can help avoid costly research efforts. In addition, the same reports can be of substantial value in justifying a decision to those making the request for expenditures.

Epilogue

An epilogue is included in this hypothetical case study to highlight some of the discoveries that MIS professionals have shared with me in the management of their distributed enterprise.

The above analysis resulted in the following actions and decisions:

- Given the timing of the downtime and considerable disruption (identified while calculating the above support effort) to the 700 users who require component upgrades, the finance department decided to postpone the Spreadsheet upgrade for now. Regardless of cost, any such disruption would have to be scheduled for the early summer months.

- The original reason for requesting the upgrade was centered on compatibility issues. As a result, users experiencing compatibility issues were upgraded to Spreadsheet 4.5, which did not require extensive hardware upgrades.

- As a result of this exercise, an IT Asset Analysis (see Case Study 2) for the finance department was run. This analysis revealed the need for a scheduled technology upgrade that would include some form of spreadsheet standardization. This upgrade was scheduled for the summer months.

From Theory to Application

This case study highlights the utility of the analysis portion of an asset tracking system. It would seem to ignore the other critical components of asset tracking, such as maintaining historical snapshots, the audit function, ad hoc reporting, and end-user transparency. In the real world, however, much of what was discussed in this case study would require all components outlined in this chapter in order to realize all benefits outlined in the case study.

Specifically, many of the targeted questions that are raised as a result of running the analysis in Case Study 3 would be answered via an ad hoc query/reporting system. If this system fails to make the asset repository accessible to all levels of those using the analyses, then the analyses will do nothing more than generate an ever-growing number of unanswered questions.

Maintaining multiple snapshots (history) of each workstation and server allows those planning the future, via historical trends, to anticipate future requirements. In this case study, how valuable would it be to know that the rest of the corporation is moving away from the Spreadsheet Inc. product, or that the finance department is slowly migrating toward an operating system or application that is incompatible with Spreadsheet 6.0?

Once a stable spreadsheet platform is established in the finance department, it must be maintained or the investment in stability is lost. An automated audit function could be set up to catch any configuration or application anomalies that might affect the compatibility or performance of the selected spreadsheet application.

These examples, and more, are successful extensions of the single analysis highlighted in Case Study 3 with each component supporting and adding value to the other. And supporting all of this functionality is the critical ease-of-use and ease-of-administration issue. If the asset tracking system is to be effective, it must not burden the user or the administrator. For every unit of complexity that is added to a broad-based information resource, such as an asset tracking system, three units of utility are lost. It is not complexity that makes a system powerful, but utility and application.

CHAPTER 6
• UTENSILS AND ROMANCE •

Me: *(After traveling more than an hour without seeing another living soul)* Where are we?

Beautiful Companion: We, Mr. "Type A" business executive, are at the world's most perfect picnic spot! See, we have the requisite grove of walnut trees, the babbling brook, a grassy bank for the picnic blanket, and a sunny seventy-eight degrees!

Me: *(After setting up the picnic site)* And what do we have for lunch?

Beautiful Companion: Fresh-baked French bread, a warm wheel of Brie cheese, crisp sliced apples, cold boneless Cornish hens with cranberry glaze, and...a very expensive bottle of your favorite Chardonnay.

Me: You mean...

Beautiful Companion: *(Holding up the bottle)* That's right, your favorite vintage.

Me: Let the picnic begin! Hand me the corkscrew.

Beautiful Companion: Corkscrew?

To be honest, it still turned out to be a wonderful picnic; but it would have been even better if we had celebrated with that exquisite bottle of wine. The wine in this case was a catalyst, having the ability to raise the value of everything it touched. Now, I would not put an asset tracking system in the same league as a near-perfect bottle of Chardonnay, but it does share the Chardonnay's ability to make associated assets more valuable.

There is a wide range of enterprise assets that have the potential not only to gain value, but to multiply value as a result of having access to an asset tracking system. A partial list of these assets that benefit from the value multiplier include: help desk systems, capacity planning tools, software distribution tools, network planning tools, change management tools, business applications, fixed-asset accounting systems, and facilities planning and maintenance systems.

The remainder of this chapter is devoted to a brief discussion of how asset tracking can further empower these applications, and it defines the qualities that an asset tracking system must have to make such empowerment possible.

EMPOWERING ASSETS

HELP DESK SYSTEMS

Since several examples have already shown how an asset tracking system can add value to a help desk service, I will forego the utility portion of this discussion. Mechanically, however, there is a great opportunity to improve productivity of the help desk application, the help desk professional, and the end user if the asset tracking system can be integrated into the help desk application. By extracting a subset of the asset tracking information and loading it into the relevant data structures of the help desk application, the analysis and tracking functions of the help desk application can include a detailed knowledge of the asset that is in question.

In reverse, it may be desirable to load portions of the help desk system into the asset tracking repository (assuming your help desk application has an export facility). With this information in the asset tracking system, you would be able to ask questions about your distributed asset base and relate them to the number or types of problems.

CAPACITY PLANNING TOOLS

Those who are involved in capacity planning have the responsibility to plan both the quantitative and qualitative aspects of the future enterprise.

Quantitatively, an asset tracking system can pass raw numbers concerning the past and current structures of the enterprise to the modeling tools used by capacity planners. Providing the capacity planning function with a current and historical analysis of the desktop and server enterprise will allow for a more accurate forecast. Qualitatively, an asset tracking system can provide capacity planning models with information such as which applications are running on which machines, or what servers have access to the sales department database. For example, it may be very important to know that 50 percent of workstations and servers in finance use the sales database.

CHARGE-BACK SYSTEMS

Because the management and support of a distributed IT enterprise is both complex and expensive, IT executives have instituted charge-back systems with the objective of tying support costs to those resources consuming support services. At the same time, end-user empowerment and the accelerating rate of change across the desktop/server enterprise have inhibited the ability to forecast and associate expenses with specific configurations and applications.

An asset tracking system that integrates with an automated charge-back system has the ability to assign a specific support cost to each desktop asset, and produce a charge-back allocation that accurately reflects the cost of supporting an individual configuration. With this capability, those managing the enterprise have the ability to "economically lead" the enterprise of users toward configurations that are cost-effective to maintain and support.

With the integration of an asset tracking system and a charge-back system in place, those making a selection of hardware, software, or combinations thereof would know that their decisions will automatically be reported to the charge-back system, and that they will be billed accordingly. This integration provides a powerful financial incentive for user departments to move toward a desired standard of maintainable configurations.

SOFTWARE DISTRIBUTION TOOLS

Part of managing the enterprise is coordinating numerous changes to distributed applications. Distributing new applications, new revisions of applications, and the coordinated distribution and collection of valuable business information in many instances are configuration dependent. By empowering an electronic software distribution system with access to an asset tracking system, you can target distributions for specific users based on their desktop configurations. In addition, a distribution can be modeled before being deployed. This modeling allows you to correct any inconsistencies between the distribution and the configuration, allowing for corrective action to be taken prior to deployment.

The link between an asset tracking system and a software distribution system has the potential to greatly reduce the time consumed by both the help desk professional and end user in correcting failed distributions. This link also makes it feasible to leverage the benefits of electronic distributions over a larger portion of the heterogeneous enterprise.

NETWORK MANAGEMENT TOOLS

A communications line goes down. As a result, your network management tool sends out alerts, begins automated recovery procedures, reports that it cannot correct the problem, and publishes a suite of network addresses that are unavailable to the enterprise. The network management staff is now charged with the task of ascertaining the problem, finding a solution, and determining the impact on business. By keeping a subset of the asset tracking repository loaded into the network management system database, or by maintaining a dynamic link between the two systems, the network management professionals, in addition to receiving network addresses, would be provided with end-user names, titles, department designations, phone numbers, critical applications that run on each affected address, and critical configuration information. With this information, the network management professionals can better establish priorities and gain insight into the impact the failure will have on business operations.

OPERATIONS CHANGE MANAGEMENT SYSTEMS

In most large enterprises, there is a group that manages changes to business operations. These individuals are responsible for evaluating and planning the movement of departments from one physical location to another, the redeployment of space, and all facets of logistics that involve physical changes. There are a number of powerful automated tools available to assist in this area. These tools track the logistics and interdependencies of all actions associated with change.

Exceptional benefits can be realized by integrating the asset repository with these change control systems. With the integration of the two systems, the change control software will be able to identify all the affected, networked users by their departments, specific physical location, and how they are attached to the network. The configuration and associated electrical power requirements can also be made available to the change system.

BUSINESS APPLICATIONS

The value of integrating an asset tracking system with business applications is dependent on the nature and structure of the business. Because a robust asset tracking system can query the end user or server administrator for information, and because the snapshots of the desktops or servers can contain non-IT information, there are infinite integration possibilities. This type of integration is less common than the types of integration listed above; however, when implemented, business integration typically offers the greatest return on investment.

FIXED-ASSET ACCOUNTING SYSTEMS

One of the most difficult tasks facing financial professionals is accounting for the distributed IT assets. The two traditional means of building a knowledge base of IT assets are: 1) a physical inventory, and 2) reconstruction of the enterprise from purchasing records. Both methods are often used by the finance department to create an accounting of the IT assets within the fixed-asset accounting system.

There are many reasons why fixed-asset accounting systems fail to accurately reflect the enterprise. These include: distributed buying authority, cannibalization of systems, unknown retirement of desktops and servers, migration of technology within and between departments, theft, and upgrades. All of these elements, and more, keep even the most diligent asset manager guessing as to the true value, type, and quantity of the assets that make up the distributed enterprise.

Linking the asset tracking repository to the fixed-asset accounting system allows for a comparison of assets by identification number, asset description, department, etc. Automated matching of the asset detail within the two systems enables the responsible party to focus on the exceptions. Clearly, the first efforts in this area will result in as many exceptions as matches; however, over time the systems will synchronize, allowing for meaningful exception handling.

Another option for solving the reconciliation issue is to use the asset tracking system as the source for the financial tracking of the IT asset base. This would require a one-time reconciliation to bring the databases into harmony; but once reconciled, the asset tracking system could automatically update the fixed-asset system as often as desired. Such an implementation is attractive because it eliminates the expense of a complete physical audit; it eliminates the reconciliation headaches encountered when assets are inventoried over a period of time; and it provides a more accurate snapshot of the distributed IT asset base.

QUALITIES REQUIRED TO EMPOWER OTHER APPLICATIONS

In writing this book, I promised myself to limit my discussion of technology to a single chapter. As this is not the chapter, I will endeavor to tie each of the empowerment (technical) attributes back to its practical application. Technical or not, the following four attributes enable an asset tracking system to reach beyond its intended purpose and extend the utility of other mission-critical functions.

HEARING FROM THE END USER

In almost all of the previous examples, there are items that cannot be discovered electronically. For example, even the best asset tracking system cannot read the asset identification sticker on the side of a monitor. The same holds true for the end-user's mailing address or the fax number nearest his or her desk. Although this information cannot be discovered electronically, it can be gathered electronically. A full-featured asset tracking system has the ability to electronically send information requests to the end user and then associate the response with either the user, desktop, or any other attribute.

Other applications and tool sets often require information that cannot be read electronically. A business application may need to know the account numbers associated with the user's activity. A help desk application may need to store some form of billing code, etc. As you think through the process of empowering other applications, you will discover that without occasionally hearing from the end user, "It is difficult to get there from here."

Things Change

No one has the ability to predict what information will be required in the future. In the case of asset empowerment, by improving the features of their products, vendors may indirectly influence what is required from the asset tracking system.

In other words, technology moves quickly. For example, several years ago it would have seemed preposterous to plan on every desktop having its own CD-ROM; today, we see it as just a matter of time. This insight brings two requirements to the forefront. First, an asset tracking system must be able to extend the range of what it discovers; and second, in adding to its reach, it must not require a reinstallation of the tracking system on the desktops and servers. If the asset tracking system is to be a true enabler, it must painlessly extend the scope of its reach across the enterprise.

The same painless extension also applies to the administration of the repository. The addition of a new item to be tracked should not require any interaction with or administration of the asset repository. As the new asset information is received, the repository should dynamically create and link the new asset item with the associated assets.

Integration Made Easy

In selecting application and tool vendors, the ability of the product to solve a problem is typically the primary buying criterion. Once the product is installed and is delivering the proposed benefit, it often becomes attractive to integrate it with other applications or business processes. Here the "vendor dance" begins. Each application/tool vendor lists the required criteria for interfacing with other applications. Then, the customer is left with the task of unraveling the file, record, and/or data structures in an attempt to create a conduit between the applications. This can be a time-consuming and expensive process, and it should come as no surprise that it generally involves the vendor's consulting group.

In the case of asset tracking systems, this process is especially burdensome because of the broad utility of the asset tracking repository. The solution is not to double your consulting budget, but to place the "data request" and/or "data delivery" burden on the asset tracking system.

REACHING THE UNREACHABLE
(THOSE NOT PART OF THE NETWORK)

When we speak of networked users, we typically include users who have a physical connection to the enterprise. There is, however, another class of users who are networked in a different manner. These users make up the business network and are often included in the scope of applications that an asset tracking system can empower. They include physically connected users, users who enter the enterprise through a public data network, and users who have no electronic connection to the enterprise.

Within the business network, users share a common mission, are part of the same organization, and/or supply a valuable service to the organization. Mobile sales professionals, suppliers, customers, and contract workers are some of the resources that may have no direct physical connection to the enterprise, but have a direct connection to the business network.

If this group of users is to be brought under the asset tracking umbrella, several extensions to traditional asset tracking methodology must be employed. First, the desktop must use an auto-inventory methodology; that is to say, the desktop must be able to inventory itself. Once this auto-inventory is complete, the asset tracking system should provide a number of methods for gathering the snapshots of the desktops and servers not connected to the physical enterprise. These methods include: automatic capture when the user accesses the Internet through a company gateway, an end-user submitted diskette, and remote server capture and transmission.

The technical details of how these capture methods work is not as important as making certain that the selected asset tracking system has the ability to capture snapshots of all users in the business enterprise. Of primary concern when considering a capture method is the routine of the end user. The more natural the collection method is to the routine of the end user, the higher the success rate will be in capturing the asset snapshots.

SUMMARY

There is no greater calling than that of making others better, for in standing near their greatness we are illuminated in their light.

CASE STUDY 4
NOW YOU KNOW

PROLOGUE

Case studies in previous chapters have centered on hypothetical organizations and their specific problems. For reasons that will be expanded upon in a moment, this case study focuses on a generic problem that is at the heart of managing every distributed enterprise—knowing what assets you have.

Whether you are a Fortune 100 manufacturer, a regional bank, an insurance carrier, a government agency, or a retail provider, you share a common challenge in managing the distributed enterprise. You are faced with the legal responsibility and business necessity of knowing the quantities and attributes of items that comprise your distributed enterprise. The question is so simple: What do we have out there? Yet for a complexity of reasons, control and knowledge of this asset base (which is often valued at hundreds of millions of dollars) is elusive, time consuming, and expensive.

ENTERPRISE DEFINITION

It would be unfair to say that all aspects of the enterprise are unmanaged. Those parts that are under the control of a single entity, such as MIS, are often some of the most accounted for assets. For example, the network of bridges and routers often falls under the dominion of a single individual or department. Here, the ordering, upgrading, and management of these resources can be tracked and controlled efficiently. Similarly, the resources in a central processing facility (mainframe) can be counted and tracked because all activity affecting them comes from a single source.

If the definition of the enterprise only included tightly managed corporate resources, the problem of accounting for enterprise assets would not exist. It is the distributed network of diverse desktops and servers that eludes management.

The Situation/Problem

It is not the attributes of the desktops and servers that make them inherently difficult to account for. It is the makeup of our business processes. A client/server architecture evolved from a need for flexibility and a need to react quickly to a rapidly changing business climate. This required empowerment of those closest to the problem. And in most cases, these individuals are not enveloped in any form of centralized enterprise reporting. In the case of managing client/server resources, this translates into a mission-critical resource having multiple sources of change, little accountability, and metamorphic consistency.

All of this is perhaps best illustrated with a diagram that highlights a single desktop and the sources and types of change that may affect its definition as a corporate asset.

Within this complexity of multiple sources and types of change, the need for basic accountability remains unchanged. How many do I have? What do they look like? And where are they located? Organizations spend millions of dollars ($42–$82.50 per desktop) every year trying to answer these questions through an annual physical inventory. What's more, these costs often do not include the agonizing effort of attempting to reconcile an inventory across a base of assets that took several months to count, while experiencing significant purchasing and business activity.

THE FIRST STEP

Shortly after implementing an asset tracking solution, assuming you make a proper selection, you will be able to produce an accurate listing of each desktop and server that makes up the enterprise. Collected information includes: the processor type and speed, attached peripherals, add-on cards, software, division, user information, memory complement, and associated server information.

From this baseline of data, you can now generate departmental and division summaries, counts by item type, and a periodic listing of all new items discovered by the asset tracking system. After multiple snapshots have been taken, you can identify equipment and software that are reported as missing and/or retired.

By collecting the newly reported software and equipment data on a cycle that matches interim financial and operating reports, management can track the growth of the enterprise against planned expenditures. By having a current picture of distributed asset activity, management can proactively manage growth in the client/server base around an annual plan, rather than discovering massive overruns at year-end.

Just the Beginning

Once the asset tracking system is implemented, several steps can be taken to make it an integral component of your accounting systems.

By working with your supplier of desktop systems, you can have them "burn" the invoice number into new systems that are shipped to your organization. This reference number would always appear on the desktop at the same location, thus allowing the tracking system to find it and make it part of the snapshot for that system.

Furthermore, any new additions to a desktop (e.g., memory, software, etc.) that do not have an asset identification number and/or invoice number associated with them can be flagged, and the appropriate identifiers can be added to the repository. Tracking assets at this level creates a closed loop between the desktop, asset inventory, and purchasing systems.

Ultimately, the ideal would be to fully integrate the asset tracking system with the fixed-asset accounting system. Although ambitious, this task can be accomplished with relative ease if the selected tracking system maintains a historical base of knowledge and has an open interface to other applications.

Epilogue

An epilogue is included to highlight some of the discoveries that MIS professionals have shared with me in the management of their distributed enterprise.

As a result of implementing an automated asset tracking system, organizations can:

• Reduce the cost of physical inventories from $55 per workstation to zero. In a 10,000-workstation enterprise, this results in a $550,000 savings.

- Proactively track the implementation of distributed IT assets during the year and react to unfavorable purchasing activities (trends) in real time, thereby avoiding year-end budget surprises.

- Give operating management a more precise view of its business operations via departmental/division summaries of distributed IT assets. This allows management to apply the same business metrics to the distributed IT asset base that it applies to other assets.

- Gain a powerful tool in monitoring the activity and integrity of suppliers by linking ("burning" the invoice number into newly ordered systems) them to the asset tracking system. In addition, the tracking of warranty status and installation certification becomes an automatic by-product of the asset tracking solution.

CHAPTER 7
• NEW DISHES •

Judi (my wife): *(Coming home from the store)* You wouldn't believe how much money I saved!

Me: What did you buy?

Wife: New dishes. They were 40 percent off.

Me: Were we in the market for new dishes?

Wife: No, but they were such a great deal I couldn't pass up the savings.

Me: You know honey, you may have a future in Congress.

I tease my wife about this and similar conversations, but in fairness, she really should be in charge of the congressional budget office. I tell this story, not because I have a desire to sleep on the couch tonight, but rather to make a point—an asset tracking system should not be difficult to cost justify. If it is, you never really had a need, or you are looking to justify it the wrong way. Asset tracking is a "Mack truck project." Its benefits are not subtle, and within a distributed enterprise, its cost justification is overwhelmingly persuasive.

To assist in the cost justification process, I have outlined several areas identified by IT executives as areas of substantial savings. I chose these areas because they highlight several different means of quantifying the value of an asset tracking system. Some of the sources of savings are mathematical; some are a "seat-of-your-pants analysis." In some ways the less formal sources are more instructive than their more precise mathematical cousins. These less quantitative savings obtain their informality out of necessity. If the asset tracking information were available, you could, in most cases, precisely calculate the value of acquiring an asset tracking system. Of course, this begs the question of why you would entertain this exercise if you already had an accurate asset tracking system in place.

EXAMPLES OF POTENTIAL SAVINGS/RETURNS

REDUCED COSTS IN CONDUCTING A PHYSICAL INVENTORY

At least once each year a physical inventory is conducted of all corporate assets. This inventory, according to industry consultants, costs between $42 and $82.50 per desktop, depending on the size of the enterprise, its geographic distribution, and whether the effort is managed in-house or contracted to an outside firm. This would place the cost of inventorying a 10,000-workstation enterprise at between $420,000 and $825,000. Keep in mind this is for a single inventory!

At first, these numbers may sound high; however, they fall into line when you consider the direct labor costs associated with conducting a physical inventory. Not included in these numbers are the costs of end-user involvement (lost productivity), travel costs, consolidation and reconciliation of the gathered information, logistics management costs, and the labor associated with managing the gathered data and reporting the results. Considering the labor-intensive nature of many of these tasks, many IT professionals consider a $200 figure to be more representative of the true cost of inventorying a desktop.

Vendor Management

Many organizations are at the mercy of software vendors when discussing upgrades and new application acquisitions because the vendors' records are the most reliable source of installation information available. One federal government IT executive recently told me he had ordered a 10,000-user upgrade knowing full well that only 3,000 copies were actually installed. His reasoning was simple: the vendor had the most accurate unit count, and the cost of proving them wrong was greater than paying for the incremental 7,000 upgrades.

In the above example, if we assume that the cost per desktop upgrade is $50, and further assume the IT executive is correct in his assessment that only 3,000 of the 10,000 copies would be put into production, then not having an asset tracking system results in an overpayment of $350,000 for the upgrade (7,000 unused upgrades x $50).

There are many variances to this theme and an equal number of ways to compute savings in this area. One way is to construct an average scenario and multiply it by the number of times you would encounter that scenario each year. Better yet, consider how past upgrade or purchasing decisions could have been improved with the availability of asset tracking information and extrapolate your results into future savings.

"Hidden Cost" Management

Simple actions often have complex cost implications. Most IT executives have been faced with the infamous upgrade "dribble effect." Here a fixed cost is identified for upgrading to the latest revision of a desktop application. After the upgrade is distributed to the user base, the dribble begins. The dribble is comprised of unanticipated CPU upgrades, memory upgrades, disk upgrades, and operating system upgrades. It is not unusual for the aggregate dribble expense to greatly exceed the cost of the software upgrade!

There is no set formula that can be applied across all organizations to determine how much money can be saved through the use of an asset tracking system uncovering hidden costs. However, the potential savings are substantial. Areas of savings include: the upgrades that will be canceled once the fully loaded cost is understood; the money saved through volume purchasing of the necessary upgrade components; end-user time saved from trying to make the new software work on an underconfigured system; and the end-user and staff time saved through the coordination of the desktop upgrades.

Even without a set formula for computing these savings, a conservative estimate can be computed by multiplying the "dribble effect" by a savings factor and using the result as a conservative savings benchmark. For example, if for each dollar spent upgrading application software another dollar is spent on associated dribble expenses (the dribble effect ratio, in this case, is 1:1), and if volume purchasing can reduce costs by 15 percent (savings factor), then you have enough information to compute benchmark savings. The annual "hidden cost" savings from having an asset tracking system would be computed as follows:

> (AVERAGE UPGRADE COST X DRIBBLE EFFECT RATIO) X
> SAVINGS FACTOR X THE NUMBER OF UPGRADES PER YEAR
> = SAVINGS

If the average application upgrade is $500,000, the dribble expense ratio is 1:1, the savings factor is 15 percent, and an average of six upgrades occur each year, the benchmark savings would be $450,000 per year ((500,000 x 1) x .15 x 6).

HELP DESK STAFFING COSTS

This one is easy. On average, determine how much time would be saved on the average help desk call if all configuration information was instantly available, showing snapshots of the end-user's machine before and after the problem was experienced. The computation of savings is straightforward:

> (TOTAL NUMBER OF CALLS X TIME SAVED PER CALL)
> X FULLY LOADED HOURLY RATE FOR HELP DESK
> PROFESSIONAL = SAVINGS

CHARGE-BACK CAPTURE
(MIGRATION TO A STANDARD DESKTOP)

As mentioned in chapter 6, an asset tracking system has the ability to provide the information necessary to tie support costs to those resources consuming the support services. As a result, users are naturally encouraged to migrate to supportable configurations. The computation of the benefits of this migration toward standards is subjective. The only formula I ever heard that attempted to quantify this type of savings came from an IT executive who worked for a bank. His formula is based on the belief that a standard desktop costs half as much to support as a non-standard desktop and makes the end users 20 percent more productive. Since he knew the support cost for his end users and the fully loaded end-user rate, he extrapolated the value of moving the desktop 10 percent closer to a desirable standard.

PROACTIVE MANAGEMENT OF KNOWN PROBLEMS

How often do we read in the press, hear from a software/ hardware vendor, or learn from the help desk group about a problem that will affect end-user productivity? Without an asset tracking system, it is impossible to find those users who will be affected by the known problems. Chapter 5 discusses how the audit function not only can identify users who have a problem configuration, but also can warn users who are likely to upgrade to a problem configuration. The computation of the asset tracking cost benefit in this area is computed by establishing three benchmarks.

Benchmark 1. First, how much downtime do end users experience when they encounter an unexpected problem? This is the average amount of time the end user loses before contacting the help desk; published statistics range from .75 to 1.5 hours.

Benchmark 2. Second, how much time does it take the help desk professional and the end user to identify the source of the problem? This assumes that both the help desk professional and the end user are equally ignorant of the problem source upon first contact; estimates for this benchmark range from .25 to 2.0 hours, depending on the industry and end-user mix.

Benchmark 3. Third, if an auditing function were in place as part of an asset tracking solution, how much help desk time would be required to proactively inform the end user of the problem? Notice that no consideration of the time required to fix the problem is included in this example. It is assumed that once the problem has been identified, regardless of the means of identification, the time required to fix the problem would be constant.

By estimating the number of end-user problems encountered that were previously known via the press, vendors, or help desk, and multiplying the number by the total time lost by end users and help desk staff (see Benchmark 1 and 2 above), we arrive at a total time spent on passively managed problems. Subtract from this the time required for the help desk and end user to proactively manage the same situation (see Benchmark 3 above), and you arrive at the incremental time required to passively manage the known problem set. Multiply this incremental time by the fully loaded hourly rates for both the end user and help desk professional, and you have computed the savings of proactively managing known problems.

REDISTRIBUTION OF IDLE ASSETS

One of the least considered, yet potentially powerful, uses of an asset tracking system is the discovery and redistribution of idle IT assets. Desktop systems and servers are often unofficially "taken out of service" for a variety of reasons, including: the restructuring of the business unit, employee transition, technology shifts, technology upgrades, and equipment failure. Most organizations have some form of surplus equipment depot; however, because of the dynamic nature of the business enterprise and geographic obstacles, it is difficult to maintain any form of count, location, or configuration of equipment not in service. Often, equipment is stored until obsolete or it is "cannibalized" and absorbed into the user base.

An active asset tracking system has the ability to detect when equipment does not report during its most recent snapshot window, allowing for immediate investigation as to the status of the asset. In addition, through the use of configuration flags, such as a byte count of available online storage, the tracking system can detect systems that are not currently active. This set of asset tracking features allows for the creation of a "virtual" surplus equipment depot of all unused or inactive assets. These assets can be redeployed as complete systems, tracked and redeployed as individual hardware and software components, or returned to a centralized depot for repair and/or redeployment.

The value of surplus equipment and the savings derived from maintaining an accurate accounting of inactive resources is largely organization specific. Typically, organizations that receive the greatest benefit from an asset tracking system in this area are those that have a span of user requirements for varying levels of technology. Within such organizations, finding utility for idle assets is simply a matter of identifying the business function that uses that level of technology (easy to find using an asset tracking system) and notifying that unit of its availability. Distribution of component parts is dependent on the base of technology and the plug-and-play nature of the components.

Measuring the precise cost savings from the tracking of these resources is accomplished by estimating the percentage of new software and hardware procurements that might be met via an asset recapture program. I have heard of estimates as low as .5 percent and as high as 20 percent. Depending on the nature of your business, and the value of new IT acquisitions each year, the savings can easily range from hundreds of thousands to millions of dollars.

IMPROVEMENTS IN BUSINESS OPERATIONS

As each business is unique, it is impossible to produce a formula that calculates the value of an asset tracking system as it relates to specific business operations. Needless to say, however, the greatest cost justification of an asset tracking system is found in this area. Asset tracking has the potential to allow a tighter integration of suppliers and customers into the enterprise. This can translate into improved margins, expanded market share, and more efficient business operations. A brief example of how asset tracking can be integrated into business operations is provided in Case Study 2.

STORED, LOST, OR STOLEN ASSETS

Like it or not, technology has become currency. Processors, memory chips, disk drives, CD-ROM drives, video cards, and printers have known and published cash equivalents.

A good friend of mine, who is a recognized leader in enterprise technology, recently illustrated the vulnerability of our IT asset base when he asked me the following questions: "Ounce for ounce, what is worth more, gold or that new notebook computer? Ounce for ounce, what is worth more, gold or that stack of memory chips? Would you leave a $5,000 chunk of gold sitting out on an open desk? If you did leave it there, would you check on it periodically?" Having never thought of IT assets in those terms, his questions awakened my interest in the mobility and liquidity of distributed IT assets.

As I began to make inquiries of IT professionals and other business managers, I discovered that many of them had already recognized the threat and had experienced losses. These losses came from a variety of sources, including: employees upgrading their home systems by swapping components with their work desktop; theft of components by contract employees; theft of complete desktops by cleaning service employees; and ordered, invoiced, and paid-for equipment that never found its way to the enterprise.

As discussed in chapter 3, an asset tracking system has the ability to make all parties aware that the assets are being watched, and allow you to react quickly to losses before they proliferate. The question is: How do you quantify this benefit as part of the justification of an asset tracking system? Corporate security or an outside security consultant is a good place to start, as they often have published statistics on the theft rate of various assets across industry segments. With such information available (e.g., your industry estimates a .5 percent loss of the high-tech asset base over a twelve-month period), your security expert can assist you in calculating the value of actively tracking the distributed asset base and, from this, a range of potential savings can be extrapolated.

I strongly encourage you to consider the potential savings/return from improved security for the distributed IT asset base. Consider the following: If you have 10,000 distributed desktops and servers with an average depreciated replacement value of $3,500 each and an assumed 1 percent loss rate over a twelve-month period, your losses will be $350,000.

The loss of the physical asset, however, is only the beginning. What is the associated productivity loss of the end users who lose their desktops? What is the administrative cost of purchasing the replacement, investigating the loss, and recovering the information that disappeared with the asset? These expenses can far exceed the replacement cost of the physical asset.

EMPOWERMENT OF OTHER IT ASSETS

To compute the savings/return through the empowerment of other IT assets, it is best to examine the original justification for the empowered asset and determine how the addition of an asset tracking system enhances that justification. For example, assume that part of the justification for the new help desk system installed last year was improved end-user productivity through rapid problem resolution. By using these projected savings as a base, you can calculate the incremental value of implementing an asset tracking system. More simply stated, if the benefit of quick problem resolution was calculated to improve end-user productivity by $5 million, and an asset tracking system improves response by an additional 20 percent, then the empowerment provided by asset tracking would logically be valued at $1 million.

SUMMARY

Valuing knowledge is an art, valuing utility is a science, but insight defies valuation, for its wisdom enriches all that rests within its grasp.

• ALUMINUM SIDING •

Me: So what kind of money are we talking about?

Aluminum Siding Salesman: How does $486 sound?

Me: For both the front and back gables?

Aluminum Siding Salesman: Yes.

Me: Sounds great. When can you begin?

Aluminum Siding Salesman: If you sign a contract today, I can have a crew out here Monday. Just sign here…

Me: Do I get to read it first?

Aluminum Siding Salesman: It's just a standard sales agreement.

Me: What does "plus installation and transport fees" mean?

Aluminum Siding Salesman: It means there is a small additional fee for those items.

Me: And what are those fees?

Aluminum Siding Salesman: There is a standard $500 installation fee for a job this size and a nominal $90 shipping fee.

Me: I think you had better nominal yourself off my property.

The contractor I eventually selected to install the siding charged me a flat $500; his contract was my promise to pay him if he did a good job. The simplicity of this transaction died twenty years ago. Today, we are faced with a bewildering cascade of options as we consider even the most basic of buying decisions. Suppliers of goods and services, in their zeal to attract profitable business, design and package items in an ever-more-confusing manner.

Today, even simple items like a car advertisement contain qualifiers that are worthy of a Mideast peace negotiation. "Drive this beauty home for $219 per month!" the ad screams in 120-point type. Down below in nine-point type, we read "(required advance payment of $1,380, 48-month closed-end lease, assumes 8,000 miles per year, customer responsible for lease origination, title, taxes, dealer prep, transfer, and delivery fees)." I have a real ambivalence about the fine print in these ads—I'm happy they are providing disclosure, but sad that disclosure is necessary.

This chapter is my capitulation to the current system; it is the small print that should appear at the bottom of every asset tracking proposal. It discloses the potential hidden and other costs associated with implementing an asset tracking system. Unfortunately, my depth of expertise and the targeted size of this book force me to document only a partial list of disclosures. I encourage you to look beyond these considerations when calculating the true cost of ownership, as the unique nature of your business or enterprise may generate issues that have an equally profound impact on the total cost of implementing an asset tracking system.

Before moving to a panorama of considerations (disclosures), it is useful to define the universe of asset tracking systems. Asset tracking systems are generally priced on a per-seat (desktop/server) basis, with licenses ranging from $15 per seat to $250 per seat. A logical assumption would be that the more expensive products offer a richer set of product features or an overall lower cost of ownership; however, some of the lower-priced solutions lay claim to these distinctions.

So what do you get for the higher price? In some cases you get "customization" that is unique to your business. In some cases you get "customization" that provides features already available in lower-priced products as a standard. And in some cases you receive extensive installation support and/or leasing services. All of this can be confusing, and if it were not, this chapter would be unnecessary. The remainder of this chapter provides a list of considerations, which, if addressed, will force vendors to reveal many of the hidden and associated costs that are inherent in the purchase and implementation of their products.

CONSIDERATIONS

HIDDEN SOFTWARE UPGRADES

The biggest hidden cost of implementing an asset tracking system is the cost of upgrading the enterprise to support the application. Some operating system vendors and network management vendors offer attractive pricing on the asset tracking component; however, when all the prerequisites are considered, the pricing is no longer so attractive.

To avoid this surprise, a list of the recommended (not minimal) "supporting" or prerequisite software should be supplied in writing by each vendor early in the decision process. In some cases, the cost of "application enabling" (upgrading) the network is five times the cost of the asset tracking application. Before dismissing the potential impact of this hidden cost, ask yourself the following question: What would it cost to upgrade the operating system on all of my servers? Don't forget the cost of the upgrade, testing, installation support, and training.

HIDDEN HARDWARE UPGRADES

Closely tied to the cost of hidden software upgrades is the associated cost of hardware required to implement those upgrades.

Even smart buyers who uncover and include the cost of the software prerequisites often fail to consider the implications that software has on the hardware resources. Typically, this is not caught during benchmarking or testing of the asset tracking system because the testing is run in a lab environment on a dedicated machine. The performance flaw in hardware configuration is not discovered until the upgraded software and asset tracking application are put into production and an incremental load is placed on the distributed servers and workstations. The solution is to load all of the required software on two production servers and their associated workstations, and then test the viability of the existing hardware and proposed software. Obviously, any hardware upgrades become part of the cost base when considering various asset tracking solutions.

Tools Versus Solutions

Some of the most expensive asset tracking systems are tools, not solutions. They deliver a framework of functionality that is tailored to the requirements of the customer. On the surface, these solutions appear to have an attractive purchase price, but in reality, the application is a Trojan horse for the vendor's consulting group. In many cases, the delivered "customized capabilities" are standard features in competitive products, and thus you end up paying premium rates for standard features. In addition, as this type of implementation is typically built on a proprietary architecture, it has the added disadvantage of tying you to a specific consulting resource. Should you decide to implement an asset tracking solution around this paradigm, at a minimum, you should make certain that the tool set is sufficiently documented and accessible to allow for competitive bids for any future customization of the product.

TRAINING PROGRAMS

Here is a case where comprehensive is not desirable. An extensive training program that is included as part of an asset tracking proposal should raise a red flag. Remember: ideally, an asset tracking system should be transparent to the end user and server administrator, intuitive and easily "tuned" by those responsible for the system, and should require little or no administration. Any training provided should be primarily directed toward those installing and modifying the system. Extensive training requirements outside these two exceptions are cause for investigation.

ASSET TRACKING SYSTEM PRICING

There are three basic components of asset tracking pricing: the cost of the software, the cost of maintenance, and the cost of updates/upgrades. Each should be considered when computing the cost of a system.

Typically, the software costs are structured around workstation pricing. Within this structure, there are variances, including: renewable twelve-month licenses, metered usage, perpetual licenses, and fees that are tied to other services such as leasing. Beware of asset tracking solutions that are tied to other services as they may hide substantial costs within other services. For example, a leasing service may provide some limited asset inventory information as part of a leasing service. This may be cost-effective as long as the leasing rates are attractive; however, should you be forced to accept higher lease rates in return for having access to asset information, you may end up paying a premium rate for an inferior asset tracking solution.

Since asset tracking is at the heart of enterprise management, the structure and price of a maintenance program must be considered. Types of maintenance programs include: per-minute support fees, annual maintenance fees based on the size of the installed base of desktops, and dedicated on-site support. Care should be taken to equalize support offerings as levels of service vary from vendor to vendor. Typically, levels of service revolve around some combination of patches (bug fixes), maintenance releases, and enhancement releases (new revisions).

Of special consideration when evaluating pricing of a maintenance program is the cost of new releases, because the pace within the IT enterprise mirrors the product life cycles of the components it tracks. As new hardware, software, and peripherals are introduced to the market and are added to the enterprise, the selected system must be enhanced to recognize and report on those new components. Given the frequency of change, it is highly desirable to have these enhancements included within the maintenance fee. In some cases, such as those systems that are based on a consulting paradigm, this will not be possible as each change requires a consulting effort. If new releases are not bundled into a flat-fee maintenance program, care should be taken to include the cost of multiple annual updates as part of the price evaluation.

Deployment and Update Costs

As a general rule, you can expect the cost of deployment to exceed the cost of the application. The initial installation of the product may be as simple as having the end user insert a diskette into the desktop, or as complex as sending out an IT professional to install and reconfigure each desktop and server. The effort required, and the associated costs of this initial installation, can be easily ascertained during product evaluations and should be included in any product price comparisons.

More important than the cost of initial installation is the cost of applying updates to the desktops. As new revisions of the asset tracking software are released, allowing for the tracking of new software and technology, the cost of performing updates becomes significant. There is a substantial variance in the cost and effort required to perform updates. Some systems automatically update the desktops and servers as part of taking a snapshot of the enterprise, while other systems require an IT professional to install and reconfigure the update on each desktop and server. Considering that each desktop may need to be updated several times each year, the effort and expense associated with each update should receive special consideration.

Cost of Integrating Results

Some asset tracking systems do not automatically create a central repository of the enterprise assets. Systems with this architecture (e.g., LAN-based asset tracking solutions) require some form of consolidation and reconciliation of the asset information that is collected from the various collection points. Depending on the tool set provided for this consolidation, the size of the enterprise, and the frequency of collection, substantial resources may be required to track and merge collection points into a central repository. Costs involved in this calculation include the time expended by the IT professionals managing the central collection effort and the time expended by those reading the data at the various collection points.

If you are considering a LAN-based asset tracking solution to manage your enterprise, special care must be taken in the administration of the solution. The consolidation of the information from the various collection points must be coordinated and verified to avoid duplication of asset information or corruption of the repository. If this is your selected methodology, it would be wise to dedicate experienced staff to the reconciliation effort.

Cost of Custom Reporting

As mentioned in chapter 6, the real value of an effective asset tracking system lies in the accessibility of the information. Accordingly, the cost of extracting that information should be considered. If each individual using the system must rely on a consultant or IT professional each time an information need falls outside the provided standard reports, the cost of providing these resources must be quantified. There is a full range of possibilities in this area—from systems that provide novice users with almost unlimited reporting capabilities to systems that have closed data structures and do not allow for non-standard reporting.

COST OF DATA ACCESSIBILITY
(EASY TO UNDERSTAND AND ACCESS)

Ideally, the asset repository would be a relational database that is open database compliant (ODBC), allowing unlimited flexiblity in the formatting and extraction of information. At the other end of the spectrum is a closed, fixed-format architecture that is accessible only by the vendor supplying the application. This issue may seem like a technical detail, but it is quintessential to establishing the cost of utility. Flexible access to the asset tracking repository is critical to empowering other applications, developing ad hoc inquiries, modeling, and auditing the enterprise. The greatest cost of not having easy access to the asset tracking repository is the inability to extract the information required to make an informed decision.

The frustration of "information starvation" takes two primary forms: first, the information is not available, and second, the time and resources required to extract the information obviates its utility.

To determine the accessibility of an asset tracking repository, ask the vendor giving the demonstration to show you how to produce (extract) several different types of information that are not part of a standard query or reporting facility. If this requires extensive vendor support, you should build substantial consulting fees into the cost model. If the information cannot be produced, you should consider another asset tracking system.

THE COST OF CHANGE

The "required information" extracted from and associated with the desktops and servers is a moving target. As new technology is implemented, business practices change, organizations evolve, and new enterprise management tools are deployed. As a result, the definition of what must be discovered, tracked, and associated with the desktops and servers undergoes a metamorphosis. The cost of making these changes should be considered when selecting an asset tracking system.

The greatest cost in this area is not that of making the change, but rather the inability to make the necessary additions and modifications to keep the repository in harmony with the organization. This inability can result in the asset tracking system becoming unable to conform to the structure of your business (e.g., a new division code cannot be associated with the desktops), unable to collect the information that enables other applications, or unable to report on a critical new piece of technology that is being added to the enterprise.

Determining the cost of modifying the system requires that you address three different types of change. First, investigate the internal and external resources required to add a new Phantom Comparative Anchor (see chapter 3) to the information associated with the desktop or server. Second, investigate the internal and external resources required to recognize a new physical asset (e.g., a new communications card) that is being deployed throughout the enterprise. And third, investigate the internal and external resources required to recognize and report on a new software package that is being deployed across the enterprise. Questions that need to be addressed for each of the three types of change include the following: Are such modifications possible? Are they practical? Can your MIS staff make these changes? Is there a documented standard that allows you to competitively outsource the changes? And, what is required to integrate these changes into the asset repository?

Don't forget that once you make these changes, you need to deploy them across the enterprise. Make certain each type of change discussed above is included in your analysis of "Deployment and Update Costs" covered earlier in this chapter.

COST OF ADMINISTRATION

Depending on the answers to the questions raised in this chapter and technology considerations (see chapter 10), the cost of administering the system may or may not be a significant factor. Primary areas of concern in determining administration cost include: the amount of end-user involvement, the amount of server administrator involvement, the effort required to change the system, frequency of changes to the system, the outside resources required to maintain the system, and the ease of extracting and transferring meaningful information to other applications and to decision makers.

The quantification of administration costs should be one of the final steps in your evaluation. After you complete your other analyses, make a list of the features, functions, justifications, and architectural components of the considered asset tracking system. Beside each line item, indicate the required administrative effort. With this list you can build an administration cost estimate.

SUMMARY

The true cost of an item is not discovered in its price, but in its use.

CHAPTER 9
• MTV STUDY GUIDE •

Me: What are you doing?

Rachel (my daughter): Homework.

Me: Why is the TV on?

Rachel: It helps me study.

Me: What are you watching?

Rachel: MTV.

Me: How does that help you study?

Rachel: It's complicated. You wouldn't understand.

Me: What are you working on?

Rachel: Algebra…I'll turn it off.

It seems silly that my daughter Rachel would view MTV as some form of a study aid, as the MTV format is by design a fast-paced, free-form, quick-cutting montage of movement and color designed to capture and hold your attention. Who but a fifteen-year-old could possibly consider this a productivity tool?

As we muse at Rachel's lack of perspective, we should be cautious in our derision, for we decision makers of Corporate America are putting an MTV competitor on the desktops in our enterprises. It too goes by three initials—WWW (World Wide Web). To eliminate confusion between the terms "Internet" and "Intranet," I will refer to the Internet as the WWW throughout the remainder of this text.

I know how unpopular it is to question the boundless productivity offered by the WWW, yet dozens of senior executives have confided in me that one of their greatest productivity problems is the misuse of this very resource.

To be certain, the WWW is a tool with vast potential; however, this potential is sharpened on both edges. As obviously as the positive aspects of the WWW present themselves, the flaws are equally good at hiding. To understand the impact that uncontrolled end-user access to the WWW can have on an organization, consider the following:

An average user, with a fully loaded cost of $105 per hour who spends twenty minutes per day surfing the WWW on non-job-related topics, will cost his employer $8,750 per year in unproductive expense. Multiply this by 10,000 Web-empowered employees, and even this moderate case of "Web waste" results in an unproductive salary expense of more than $87 million! This doesn't even account for the cost of lost productivity (lost opportunity cost), which could easily triple the impact.

Because of the "richness" of WWW resources, employees are increasingly overresearching even the simplest information needs. I recently asked one of my senior managers to find out the annual revenues of a prospective business partner. My need to know this information was driven by my desire to mentally slot them into one of our existing programs. By knowing their current revenues, I could easily determine the level of resources they would consume and the type of training they would require.

Several hours later, the senior manager returned with a stack of paper three inches thick on the company in question. Included in this stack of information were sections that had been marked with a highlighter and numerous notes in the margin. This manager, empowered by the MTV-like flash of the WWW, had explored the WWW for my answer and found the jewel I desired, as well as a vast treasure of information not requested. The price of this excursion was more than $500 in unproductive expense.

The WWW also has the power to diminish the productivity of those individuals who use discipline in their WWW activity or who do not use the WWW at all. In the above example, the senior manager overresearched a simple data request, wasting $500 of salary and productivity expense. The impact of this waste did not end there, however, for he sent copies of his research to three other managers including me. Much to my regret, I skimmed the entire packet of information, actually reading the highlighted areas and margin notes. I later discovered the other managers did the same. In the final analysis, I did get the revenue number I requested, but at a dear price. Collectively, the two other senior managers and I spent one and a half hours reading information that was not requested and that was of limited value. Each of us would have been far more productive spending that time on our core jobs.

The total price tag for this single effort of overresearch was more than $800. If this seems like an anomaly to you, I would encourage you to look at the number of attachments to your e-mail traffic. E-mail is the perfect carrier for this infectious waste of productivity, and most of us find it difficult not to pop open those attachments when sent from someone we respect.

One of the most fascinating aspects of the WWW is that its availability is predicated on self-interest, rather than profit. That is to say, providers of information on the WWW do not do so in order to promote the WWW or receive a royalty; instead, they have a single selfish interest—to make their "story" (information) available to others.

This availability of free information often positions the WWW as a source of news and reference material. In many cases this label is accurate, but increasingly, organizations are discovering that much of the research extracted from the WWW is biased and/or highly suspect. If we detach ourselves from the Web hysteria for a moment, the reason for all of the suspect information is obvious. There is no profit motive to keep things honest.

Every credible news source has an underlying need for accuracy. If they report false information on a regular basis, the public will stop buying their product and they will cease to exist. Not so on the WWW where anyone who has a point of view can publish an opinion that may be masked as a research document encased in credentials nearly impossible to verify.

As a result, organizations are increasingly monitoring the information sources used by their employees. This monitoring is targeted toward two objectives. First, to ensure the organization has an accurate base of facts on which to make a decision. And second, to prevent their most valuable assets, their employees, from wasting time with resources that will later be discounted—or worse yet—lead to wrong decisions.

End-user productivity is increasingly tied to the network of clients and servers known as the Intranet. The Intranet is the internal web of communications lines, bridges, routers, and modems that allow these clients and servers to communicate at high speeds (e.g., 1.5 million bits per second).

Joining the internal Intranet to the outside world of the WWW is a gateway. This gateway allows internal users, attached to the Intranet, to access the "free" outside resources of the WWW. The diagram on the following page begins to illuminate how this "free resource" can cost an organization millions or even tens of millions of dollars each year.

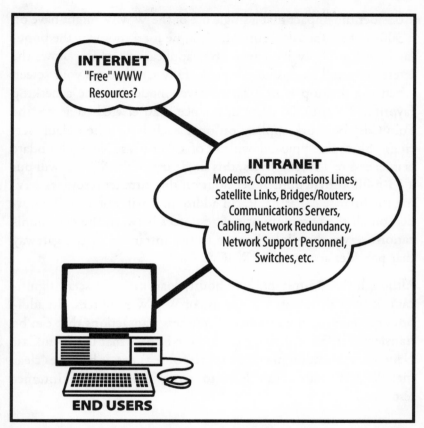

This diagram highlights the vast resources separating the users from the WWW. This conglomeration of resources, the Intranet, is responsible for carrying the traffic of the organization's mission-critical applications. Organizations spend vast sums of money to ensure that there is bandwidth to carry this mission-critical traffic and to provide a rapid response to its end users.

The same resources that carry the mission-critical traffic also carry extraneous Internet traffic. Thus, many organizations that are not in control of Internet usage find themselves with unexplained degradation of their Intranet, and are forced to upgrade Intranet resources in an effort to maintain adequate response times and throughput for mission-critical applications.

Consider the impact that a single use of the WWW might have on a 300-user finance department. Assume for a moment the popular PointCast Network screen saver application, which allows the latest news and stock quotes to colorfully scroll across your screen when the desktop is in a screen saver mode, became a desktop favorite. Of the 300 users in finance, 220 elected to access the PointCast Network application once each hour (the default setting). Since the typical download of a PointCast Network update is in excess of 150,000 bytes, this single use of the WWW will put a 33-million-byte burden per hour on the Intranet resources serving the finance department. In addition, it will put a similar burden on all the communications resources between the communications server that links finance to the Intranet and the gateway that provides access to the WWW.

Although this 33-million-byte hourly load may not seem significant, it only represents a single use of WWW resources. In addition, considering the number of business transactions that can be transferred in 33 million bytes, and the impact that the PointCast Network application may have on response times, it becomes clear that WWW traffic can lead to costly upgrades of Intranet resources.

TAMING THE NET

This discussion may lead you to believe that I am against plugging users into the WWW. Although it is true that some users would be well served by having their access to the WWW blocked, I am a strong proponent of making the WWW available to the majority of users. This assumes there are reasonable controls in place, allowing policies to be monitored and enforced. In reality, the WWW is a resource not unlike a long-distance phone service. Not all callers need access to the WWW, just as not all callers need access to international long-distance service.

If reasonable control of the WWW is to be exercised, you must be able to:

1) Associate WWW traffic with individual users.

2) Understand trends in WWW usage.

3) Determine what WWW resources are being used.

If this information is known, the WWW can be used with few or none of the problems discussed earlier. It should not be surprising that an effective asset tracking system can be invaluable in gathering and presenting actionable WWW usage analyses.

WEB FINGERPRINTS

As mentioned earlier, access to the WWW is attained through the Intranet via a gateway. This gateway, in addition to providing access to the WWW, records the activity that passes through it. This activity log would be nothing but a numeric jumble of transactions of fingerprints if it were not for the asset repository. The asset repository can apply these transactions to individual users, departments, or divisions and collect and sort them by type of activity.

An asset tracking system has the ability to capture and apply the raw data fingerprints left behind by WWW activity. This raw fingerprint data includes: the time of day the WWW request was made, the network address making the request, the site accessed (e.g., Disney, General Motors, SEC), all pages (specific pieces of information from the site), and the number of bytes transferred as a result of each query. In processing this amalgamation of information, the asset tracking system sorts and associates each transaction with the existing base of knowledge on workstations, servers, and end users. Once processed, the asset tracking system presents its results from several different perspectives, enabling proactive control of both user productivity and network productivity as they relate to WWW activity.

UNDERSTANDING WWW ACTIVITY

To understand the meaning of WWW activity, you must focus on five factors. Each of these factors, separately and in combination, is required to effectively manage WWW activity. These factors include:

1) *What sites are being accessed?* This information includes not only the top sites accessed by the organization, department/division, and individual, but also the number of different sites being accessed. Here is the best macro-measurement of how the WWW is being used: Is the number one site for your finance department Dow Jones or Disney?

2) *What pages are being requested?* Here the specific information that your users are consuming is discovered. The most frequently accessed site by your marketing department may be the *Wall Street Journal*, but if 80 percent of the accesses to this site are for the sports scores page, you may not be getting the desired utility out of your WWW resources.

3) *What time is the WWW activity taking place?* It has been said that timing is everything, and WWW usage confirms this axiom. Knowing that your sales department has a substantial number of accesses to an interactive golf simulation page may not be disturbing if accessed during lunch hours, but may be unacceptable at 3:00 P.M. The timing of WWW activity is especially critical when network issues are being addressed.

4) *What is the trend of WWW activity?* Almost all WWW activity is best viewed across time. Is usage over time on the increase, or is this month's activity an anomaly?

5) *How much information is being transferred?* A user in the shipping department may only access the Disney site four times per month; however, each access may result in the downloading of 20-million-byte animation files during peak traffic hours.

These five factors provide the keys to understanding the utility of the WWW within your organization. The power of combining these factors with other information in the asset tracking repository is best illustrated in Case Study 5.

SUMMARY

It is a half-educated man who sees opportunity in adversity while ignoring the mishap of good fortune.

CASE STUDY 5
SNARED IN THE NET

Prologue

RMS Capital is a worldwide firm providing financial services to major corporations. Its services include leasing, facilities management, and financial advisory services. Because RMS Capital's business is based solely on employee productivity, a senior manager roundtable is held each quarter to explore ways to improve employee productivity. The meeting is held in turn, with each senior manager having the opportunity to host and control the topics of discussion. This meeting is chaired by Susan Chin, chief information officer for RMS Capital.

Enterprise Definition

RMS Capital has an enterprise of approximately 18,000 desktops that are connected via 3,400 servers. The network consists of a home-office site that represents 14,000 of the desktops with the balance of the units distributed across twenty-three regional worldwide facilities.

Because RMS Capital's business relies on information-based financial services, it values the power of automation and devotes a substantial portion of expenditures to maintaining and upgrading IT resources. Two such upgrades—implementation of an asset tracking system and providing users with access to the WWW— were implemented within the past year.

The Situation/Problem

Although RMS Capital is growing, its rate of growth and sales productivity have declined in the two most recent quarters. Reasons attributed to this decline include: increased competitive pressures, weak product positioning, a change in the sales force compensation package, and the economy.

Other departments within the company have experienced similar sags in their productivity numbers. It is for these reasons that Susan Chin has decided to focus this quarter's roundtable on encouraging departments to use the WWW as a means of boosting productivity.

THE FIRST STEP

Susan begins by running a series of analyses on WWW activity for the most recent months. She suspects that employees may be timid about using the Internet, which is causing them to fall behind their competitors. The information highlighted in the analyses is not what Susan expected. In fact in some cases the WWW seems to be overused, resulting in decreased productivity. Susan decides to focus the entire roundtable session on productivity issues surrounding the WWW.

TRACKING DOWN THE PROBLEM

Susan calls the meeting to order, announcing the agenda and distributing copies of the first analysis. *Note: The format of this book prohibits reproduction of this analysis in a single-page format. The analysis has been divided on the following pages section by section.*

INTERNET ACCESS ANALYSIS — SUMMARY

The first section of the Internet Access Analysis displays summary information on page and site activity. With more than 7.8 million page accesses for the current month, all managers gain an understanding of how pervasive WWW use has become within RMS Capital.

SUMMARY

There are 13,449 workstations that report Internet activity during the specified period. These workstations connected to 10,659 sites and accessed 7,825,693 pages, including 2,738,993 unique pages.

INTERNET ACCESS ANALYSIS — USAGE BREAKDOWN

Once this information is known, the next logical question is, who is using it? The analysis anticipates this question, providing an insightful usage table.

INTERNET USAGE						
DEPARTMENT	FINANCE	IT	MKTG	SERVICE	SALES	ADMIN
TOTAL WORKSTATIONS (#)	3887	1866	2644	933	3420	2799
TOTAL WORKSTATIONS (%)	25%	12%	17%	6%	22%	18%
WORKSTATIONS ON THE INTERNET(%)	100%	90%	100%	15%	100%	60%
PAGE ACCESSES (#)	2034680	1408625	939083	0	2973763	469542
AVG ACCESS PER WORKSTATION (#)	523	839	355	0	869	280
PAGE ACCESSES (% OF TOTAL)	26%	18%	12%	0%	38%	6%
UNIQUE PAGES (#)	712138	493019	328679	0	1040817	164340
UNIQUE SITES (#)	2503	1733	1155	0	3658	578
TOP TEN USERS (%)	50%	80%	40%	0%	90%	30%

It is from this table that Ben Houser, vice president of sales, discovers the first anomaly concerning WWW usage. Ben points out that although his group makes up only 22 percent of the workstation population (line 2), they make up 38 percent of all WWW page accesses (line 6). Clearly, sales has a high activity level on the WWW. Other managers identify additional areas of interest, but Ben, citing the recent drop in sales productivity, directs them back to his group's issue. He notes that ten of his users are especially active in that they make up 90 percent of all pages accessed by sales (line 9).

Since sales productivity has been such a priority at RMS, everyone agrees to explore the sales department's use of the WWW before considering other WWW issues.

INTERNET ACCESS ANALYSIS — HOURLY PAGE ACCESS

Ben's next question deals with timing, as his group often works on proposals in early morning and late evening hours. Addressing this question in the following section, the analysis displays the month's page activity by department across a twenty-four-hour period.

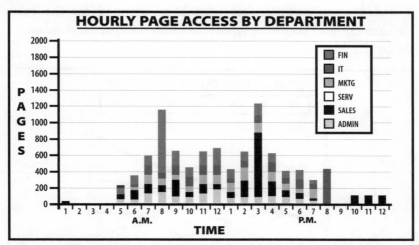

Reviewing this chart, Ben discovers no heavily weighted sales department use at the beginning or end of the days, but rather a fairly uniform distribution. He also discovers an extraordinary spike in page accesses at 3:00 P.M. This is especially unusual because this is the time of day he expects his staff to be in front of the customer. Ben decides to investigate the reason for the spike at 3:00 P.M. and the unusual activity between 10:00 P.M. and midnight.

INTERNET ACCESS ANALYSIS — DEPARTMENTAL PAGE ACCESS

Realizing these results may be a function of some special project or circumstance, Ben consults the next section of the analysis that highlights a six-month trend in usage for each department.

In reviewing the usage curves, Ben observes that, not only does he have a potential problem, but the problem is growing with each passing month. Susan concludes that most groups' use of the WWW has stabilized or declined as the novelty diminished. Ted

Dunmore, CFO, notes that the increased use in the finance department may be due to two new services recently made available to the financial analysts. Ben indicates that to the best of his knowledge, no new services have been acquired for the sales department and asks for a report detailing the specific page activity by department.

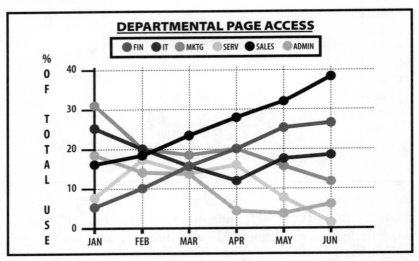

In the course of the meeting, Susan provides Ben with an analysis revealing that the majority of sales department usage is being consumed playing an interactive Space Wars game. Further investigation reveals that the Space Wars tournament started promptly at 3:00 P.M. each afternoon. Susan also produces an analysis, showing the top twenty-five consumers of pages within the company, also known as "Page Hogs." To no one's surprise, thirteen of the twenty-five "Page Hogs" were in sales.

Susan also provides all managers with additional insight into their departments' WWW usage by producing a "Site Hog" analysis and a "Network Hog" analysis. This last analysis is instrumental in clearing up a network bottleneck. The analysis reveals that the bottleneck was caused by users who were regularly downloading sexually explicit graphics during the batch distribution of operating reports across the Intranet.

Finally, Susan distributes to the appropriate managers a personal profile of usage for each employee who appears on one of the "hog" analyses. These detailed profiles reveal that more than half of the "hogs" were primarily using the WWW for personal interests.

EPILOGUE

An epilogue is included in this hypothetical case study to highlight some of the discoveries that MIS professionals have shared with me in the management of their distributed enterprise.

The above roundtable review of the WWW analyses results in the following actions and decisions:

- A formal policy is published and made part of the employee handbook. End users are informed that WWW activity is actively monitored and that appropriate action will be taken against employees violating the established guidelines for WWW usage.

- The Internet gateway is configured to block a list of sites that contain offensive or non-productive material.

- The network management group is assigned the task of reviewing the WWW network traffic analyses each month. They are charged with submitting a monthly report, recommending network-intensive sites that should be blocked and hours during which Internet access should be restricted. As a result of the recommendations, in the first sixty days of this program, two substantial network upgrades were avoided.

- Internet access is blocked from 37 percent of the desktops that failed to justify their need for Web services. The sales department reduces the number of connected users by 45 percent.

- The benefits of the WWW are reintroduced to the customer services group in an effort to give them greater access to customer information and improve customer response times. It is discovered that their decline in WWW use is tied to a network-loading conflict, which was easily resolved by rescheduling downloads during off hours.

- Sales productivity began to show substantial improvement within weeks of implementing the above policies.

FROM THEORY TO APPLICATION

In theory, all of the above outcomes were made possible by the analyses reporting on WWW activity. In reality, the success attained in managing the WWW had more to do with the basic functions of asset tracking than sorting and summarizing raw gateway data. Clearly, it was assigning this processed data to business entities (Phantom Comparative Anchors) that illuminated its meaning. It was comparing the values of the raw gateway data to other tracked information (Reflective Comparative Anchors) that provided a relative understanding of the problem. It was maintaining and associating this information over a period of time (Trends Comparative Anchor) that allowed managers to focus on escalating problems rather than apparitions. Finally, it was associating this same raw data with those consuming the WWW resources (Phantom Comparative Anchor) that allowed corrective action to be taken.

CHAPTER 10

HOUSEBOAT

Kay: *(Observing a just-finished sailboat built in her fiancee's basement)* It's beautiful!

Tom (her fiancee): It's taken me more than two and a half years to complete, but it's worth it.

Kay: Why did you decide to build a boat?

Tom: I've always loved the water, loved to work with wood, and I found these award-winning plans for this sloop.

Kay: I mean, why did you decide to build a boat here?

Tom: That's a silly question. This is my basement; this is where I have my tools. Where else would I build it?

Kay: No, I mean, how are you going to get it out of here? There's no way that boat is going up those stairs!

Tom: *(Angry)* That's a stupid question! Just leave me alone!

The young woman in this true story is my mother. This exchange happened almost twenty years before I was born, yet my mother never fails to marvel at Tom's miscalculation as she retells the story. Tom had forgotten there are many aspects of technology, whether applied to art, boat building, or distributed enterprise management. Each component of technology must be considered within the context of the mission or you run the risk of facing a very narrow set of stairs with a very wide boat.

Within the context of a mission, technology includes tools (hardware and software), skilled workers, plans/architecture, and logistics. No one of these components has the ability to make the mission successful, but any one of them can scuttle the effort. Mission components and subcomponents are sometimes obscure and sometimes so big that we are unable to focus on them.

This chapter does not attempt to define all of the technologies you must embrace if you are to successfully implement an effective asset tracking system. This would be a fool's errand, as each organization and its enterprise is comprised of a unique set of tools and objectives. Here, I only wish to introduce those items that, if not considered, will prove to be costly detours or even fatal to the mission. As a concession to my editor, I have limited these considerations to a list of eleven "Technology Dos and Don'ts." I have not prioritized these items as their priority will largely depend on the unique circumstances of each organization.

TECHNOLOGY DOS AND DON'TS

DO NOT IMPLEMENT AN ASSET TRACKING SYSTEM THAT IS NOT BUILT ON AN OPEN-DATA STRUCTURE

In the case of an asset tracking system, an ODBC database can be your key to success. The advantages of an ODBC database include:

- It provides you with full access to the repository via SQL query engines.

- It prevents you from becoming locked into a specific vendor for customization and support.

- It allows easy exporting and importing of information from other applications and support tools.

- It provides a robust set of tools to tune and maintain the integrity of the repository.

- It minimizes training and hiring requirements as ODBC-database skills are probably already present within your organization.

DO NOT IMPLEMENT AN ASSET TRACKING SYSTEM THAT DISTURBS OR CHANGES THE COMMUNICATIONS LINK BETWEEN YOUR CLIENTS (END-USER WORKSTATIONS) AND SERVERS

As asset tracking systems, by definition, must "touch" the end-user machines, great care must be taken not to negatively impact the stability of the desktops. One of the most fragile links in the productivity chain is the communications link the desktop has with its server. If a selected asset tracking system requires that special drivers be installed or that parameters of existing communications hardware and/or software on the desktop be changed, a substantial amount of uncertainty is introduced into the network.

Beware! Such changes may appear to be harmless in the lab, but when introduced in the field, they may introduce variables that create conflicts with other mission-critical applications. Arithmetic speaks volumes on this topic. A change in the communications link between the clients and servers that causes intermittent problems with just 15 percent of an enterprise population of 10,000 users, brings forth 1,500 open help desk tickets!

DO SELECT A DESKTOP DISCOVERY PROCESS THAT IS SELF-DEFINING

Regardless of the asset tracking system selected, some form of discovery (i.e., ascertaining what items make up the desktop) must take place on the desktop. This discovery process is then used to update the repository and provide the capabilities described in earlier chapters. However, what if the link to the repository is down? What if the end users have an immediate need to know configuration information about their desktops, and they do not have access to the repository? What if the users are not connected to the enterprise and wish to convey the status/configuration of their machine to those supporting them? If the selected asset tracking solution has a self-defining discovery process, users can print out or display information about their desktops in a readable/self-defining format (e.g., CPU Type = 486, Operating System = Windows 3.1, etc.).

This capability may rarely be needed, but having it can make the difference in solving a problem in minutes versus days. In addition, it empowers end users to make more intelligent decisions when considering or dealing with self-installed shrink-wrapped applications.

DO NOT SELECT AN ASSET TRACKING SYSTEM THAT IS NOT SCALABLE

Asset tracking is an evolving science. Just two years ago, tracking WWW activity was not considered fundamental to effective enterprise management. Today, any tracking solution that does not address WWW activity is less than state of the art.

It is impossible to predict what hooks and extensions will be required of an enterprise asset tracking system over the next five years; but it is certain that whatever the future holds, it will require more input/output (I/O) and processing capacity. Therefore, whatever asset tracking system is selected, it should run on a wide array of processing platforms, allowing for infinite expansion in the number of supported desktops and servers (remember mergers and acquisitions), and limitless expansion of the information it tracks and stores.

DO CHOOSE A SYSTEM THAT SUPPORTS A WIDE RANGE OF PLATFORMS AND OPERATING SYSTEMS

Typically, organizations view themselves as having standardized on a desktop platform, yet when I probe deeper, the conversation more typically goes as follows:

Me: What do your desktops look like?

IT Executive: We've standardized on Windows 95.

Me: Then 100 percent of your users are Windows 95?

IT Executive: Well, about 5 to 6 percent are Macintosh, mostly in marketing and senior management.

Me: Any UNIX or DOS desktops floating around?

IT Executive: About 8 percent of the desktops are UNIX, primarily the financial analysts and engineers. And the product providers who run a DOS-based application are around 11 to 12 percent of the population.

Me: So about 75 percent of your users are Windows 95?

IT Executive: Yeah, either Windows 95 now or they're scheduled to be upgraded over the next year from Windows 3.1 to Windows 95.

This composite conversation highlights two truths about most organizations. First, although they have a strong preference for a specific platform, it never really becomes an "enterprise standard." And second, those that fall outside the standard are often the most high-profile users. In the above example, if I had rephrased my question—So how do you feel about an asset tracking solution that excludes a large portion of your senior managers, financial analysts, product providers, and a bunch of people in your marketing department?—I suspect broad-platform support would receive serious consideration.

Even if you have an absolute standard for your enterprise, broad-platform support should still be given serious consideration. Remember that your need for it is as close as the next merger or acquisition.

DO NOT SELECT AN ARCHITECTURE THAT REQUIRES CONSOLIDATION OR RECONCILIATION OF MULTIPLE REPOSITORIES

With the proliferation of client/server applications, the distribution of information across the enterprise has become fashionable. Many applications lend themselves to this physical distribution of data, but asset tracking is not one of them. The true beauty of an enterprise-wide asset tracking solution is its ability to present an accurate model of your enterprise at any level. It provides immediate answers to questions like: Who else has this problem configuration? How do the desktops in the sales department compare to the rest of the corporation? Who is generating the most Internet-initiated traffic? The answers to these questions are available because there is a single central repository of asset information.

Beware of server-based asset tracking systems that require additional steps to generate an enterprise-wide view of your distributed IT assets. Such consolidations can be complex, time- and network-consuming, and are prone to error. In addition, because of these complexities, organizations tend to lessen the frequency of consolidations and thus decrease the utility of the tracking system.

DO SELECT A SYSTEM WITH AN EXTENDABLE ARCHITECTURE

Within this context, extendable pertains to both what is discovered and what is maintained in the repository. Specific questions that should be addressed when considering the "extendability" of the architecture include:

• When a new desktop or server is discovered, what steps, if any, need to be taken to make the appropriate entry into the repository? The repository should automatically create a new record.

• When a new component is discovered on the desktop or server, what steps, if any, need to be taken to make the appropriate entry into the repository? The repository should automatically append the appropriate desktop record.

• What steps, if any, are required to expand the discovery process to include a new device (e.g., credit card reader)? A well-documented software development kit (SDK) should be available to allow organizations to create their own discovery agents.

• Once a new discovery agent is created, what steps are required to populate the desktops and servers with the new agent? The repository should have the ability to automatically populate the enterprise with the new agent.

• Does the proposed system support interactive discovery agents (i.e., agents that query the end user and/or server administrator for information)? If so, are these agents created via the standard SDK? Can interactive agents be defeated by the end user?

DO NOT SELECT AN ASSET TRACKING SOLUTION
WITHOUT INVESTIGATING THE RANGE AND DEPTH OF
THE DISCOVERY PROCESS

Considerations include: What software, hardware components, and communications links can be identified? What operating system configuration information is discovered and tracked? Remember that each of the above questions must be asked for each client and server platform.

Questions in this area include:

• How many historical snapshots is the system capable of tracking? The amount of historical information should be limited only by the physical storage capacity of the repository machine.

• How often can snapshots be taken? There should be no limit as to how often a desktop can be inventoried. If the discovery process is transparent to the end-user and server administrators, you should consider collecting two to four snapshots each month. Note: Individual circumstances may dictate a more or less frequent schedule.

• How many desktop, network, and repository resources are required to take a snapshot of the enterprise?

• How are snapshots scheduled? Do all desktops and servers need to be on an identical schedule? You should be able to set schedules in a manner that distributes and optimizes network load.

• What steps must the end user execute to facilitate a snapshot of the desktop? Ideally, no end-user or server-administrator involvement is required.

Questions that should be addressed include:

• What automated functions are available to initially populate the enterprise desktops with the proposed system? The desktops should be populated via their attached server.

• Can new desktops automatically be populated without involving the end user or support staff? Once the servers are populated, the desktop should be populated the first time it connects into the enterprise.

- When a user accidentally or intentionally removes the tracking application from the desktop, what steps are required to reinstall the application? The software should automatically reinstall the next time the workstation connects to the network.

- What steps are required to implement the system on the enterprise servers? The server should have a point-and-click installation program that requires only the identification of the repository address.

- What skill sets are required to install and maintain the asset repository? Ideally, the repository should come fully populated with functionality and should require no custom programming or consulting. Heavy consulting-based solutions should be avoided as planning and design efforts require significant involvement from your IT staff. In addition, consulting-based solutions take longer to implement, introduce unproven concepts and codes into the solution, typically provide less functionality, and are more expensive. A properly designed asset tracking solution should require no specialized skills other than a technician capable of installing an ODBC database.

DO FOCUS ON UTILITY WHEN SELECTING AN ASSET TRACKING SYSTEM

Often when evaluating technology, we become so engrossed in the metrics of technology that we lose sight of functionality. Consider the following points when evaluating an asset tracking system:

- How broad a spectrum of users will be able to leverage the proposed system? Does the proposed system provide multiple levels of access for different types of users?

- How broad is the utility offered by the proposed solution? Does it only appeal to IT professionals or does it offer specific utility to a range of professionals (e.g., finance, purchasing, help desk, security, etc.)?

- How approachable is the proposed system (easy to use)? Regardless of utility, if it has a daunting interface, it is unlikely that nontechnical users will avail themselves of the potential benefits of an asset tracking system.

- How lucid are the results produced by the proposed system? Any system (even if it's easy to use) that produces confusing or cumbersome results will only be used by the most knowledgeable individuals.

- How much training is required to make a typical user productive? If the proposed system requires formal training before delivering recognizable benefits, it is unlikely that the system will be broadly adopted by the organization's business functions (nontechnical staff and managers). Ideally, formal training can be avoided by selecting a system that has an inviting, intuitive, and familiar interface.

SUMMARY

The primary product of technology is not results or progress or efficiency, but something much greater...opportunity.

CHAPTER 11
•   LICENSE AND   •
REGISTRATION, PLEASE

Officer: May I see your license and registration, please?

Me: Yes, sir.

Officer: Mr. Jesse, did you know that you were speeding?

Me: Yes, sir.

Officer: Any idea how fast you were going?

Me: No, sir.

Officer: You were doing 52 in a 35 mph zone. You running late?

Me: No.

Officer: Going somewhere special?

Me: Nowhere really, just going for a ride.

Officer: Well, Mr. Jesse, I appreciate your honesty, but I'm going to have to write you up. I'm afraid you're going to be a little late to nowhere, and when you get there you will be $60 lighter.

This incident, upon reflection, taught me one of the great lessons of my adult life: that time, money, and objectives are part of a balanced equation. In this case, I bought time for $60 with no reason or plan as to how to spend it and I got a bonus—two points on my license. As I discovered later in life, time also has the ability to unbalance the equation. In this case, the money and objectives are the given, but time prevents the actuation of a positive result.

I have saved this discussion for the last chapter as it highlights a problem facing you or anyone else who is empowered with the knowledge and desire to implement an effective asset tracking solution. You know what you want and are more than willing to pay the price, and yet the starting gun is silent. Here, time never becomes part of the equation, and the positive result is delayed or never realized.

In considering the concepts outlined in this book, including the compelling return-on-investment (ROI) case, why would any rational manager postpone implementing an asset tracking solution? The answer to this question has more to do with how decisions are made than the decision itself. We have created a decision process for enterprise-based products and solutions that takes a year or more to complete. It involves consultants, industry analysts, and committees, with special consideration being given to strategic vendors, reports, comparative studies, requests for proposals (RFPs), price negotiations, and trials. The result is a confusing array of technically based decision criteria that defy translation into a business case.

I am not dismissing the value of this evaluation cycle, as it was forged around years of experience and is designed to avoid failure. In the case of an asset tracking solution, however, risk aversion is not the primary aim. As we have seen in this text, the opportunity base available through implementing an asset tracking solution is so vast that even a partially effective solution has the ability to produce an extraordinary ROI. Asset tracking does not fit the traditional evaluation model of "precise implementation for marginal returns." Consequently, waiting a year or more to implement a solution is both financially and competitively unsound.

I would not be so bold as to tell you how to redesign your organization's decision process, as it is highly dependent on a myriad of factors. However, I am suggesting the following paradigm when you evaluate an asset tracking solution. Here speed replaces caution in the decision process, as the overwhelming benefits of rapid deployment vastly outweigh the advantages of a tedious investigation.

Week 1

Conduct an informal (e.g., "back-of-the-envelope") analysis of potential savings (see chapter 7). Use conservative but realistic estimates and include all areas of potential savings. This should produce a ROI case that will allow you to garner the necessary support for the next step.

Weeks 1 & 2

Prepare a business case that involves and spans a broad base of functions (e.g., finance, IT, operations, purchasing, help desk, etc.). In doing so, you build a broad base of justification and internal support so if one area fails to meet expectations, other areas will continue to justify the decision. Ways to build such a consensus include: introducing targeted individuals to the case studies and types of analyses covered in this text, arranging for some form of self-directed (e.g., video or CD-ROM) product demonstration, or providing each of them with a copy of this book.

Week 2

Verify your business case and "back-of-the-envelope" assumptions with the supporters in each of the functional groups and make appropriate adjustments if necessary.

Weeks 2 & 3

Solicit a list of "best-of-breed" solutions from a reputable industry analyst.

Weeks 3 & 4

Contact the top three vendors on the above list and compare the various offerings against a matrix of desired features (see chapters 5 and 10). *Note: I have developed a detailed evaluation document for this purpose, but space considerations prohibit me from including it in this text. For a free electronic copy of this document, drop me an e-mail at chrisj@tesi.com.*

Weeks 4 & 5

View a live demonstration (at a customer site) of the top one or two contenders.

Weeks 6 & 7

Select a solution and implement a multiserver, 250-desktop pilot. This should require minimal funding and avoid any extended sign-off cycles. Note: By having this pilot and gathering snapshots twice a day for a two-week period, you can simulate several quarters of activity over a short period of time.

Week 8

Assuming a successful pilot, seek funding for a departmental implementation and begin enterprise implementation. Note: This schedule assumes that the negotiation of the contract and pricing terms, as well as departmental funding efforts, overlap the product evaluations in weeks five, six, and seven.

This eight-week investigation to implement an asset tracking solution may at first sound radical, but it is far less extreme than letting your current base of IT assets go unmanaged for another year. Forward-thinking organizations—perhaps your competitors—are moving quickly in an effort to realize the productivity gains associated with the proactive management of their distributed IT enterprises. Perhaps the most radical concept of all is knowingly to let your competitors have a ten-month lead in such an undertaking.

And what if you discover seven weeks into the eight-week program that you should have selected an alternative product? The answer is to abandon your effort on the first product and install the second. Upon completion of the second eight-week program (implementation of the second solution) you will still only have fifteen weeks invested in implementing a successful solution. And besides, as a highly esteemed CIO once told me, "I'm not sure you have any better chance of picking a winner in twelve months than you do in eight weeks."

I opened this chapter talking about the time-money-objective equation. There is actually a fourth part to that formula—risk. Moving boldly to seize the opportunity of dramatic productivity gains requires that risks be taken. But, oh, how small they seem when compared to the prize. To be certain, there is always a hazard in moving forward, but I encourage you to embrace the chance. For you and Dorothy, in your enterprise and in Oz, shall never find your way home by standing still.